$O \frac{50}{27}$

D0520485

THE *Return*
OF *Courage*

TRANSLATED BY
FRANCES FRENAYE

Reading, Massachusetts Menlo Park, California New York
Don Mills, Ontario Wokingham, England Amsterdam Bonn
Sydney Singapore Tokyo Madrid Bogotá Santiago San Juan

The
RETURN
of
COURAGE

Jean-Louis Servan-Schreiber

ADDISON-WESLEY
PUBLISHING COMPANY, INC.

Library of Congress Cataloging-in-Publication Data

Servan-Schreiber, Jean-Louis, 1937–
    The return of courage.

    Translation of: Le retour du courage.
    1. Courage   I. Title.
BJ1533.C8S47I3   1987   179'.6   87-1:88
ISBN 0-201-12207-3

Cover design by Nancy Culmone
Text design by Copenhaver Cumpston

THE RETURN OF COURAGE was set by DEKR Corp. of Woburn, Mass., in 10/13 Linotron Galliard, a typeface designed for photocomposition by Matthew Carter.

ABCDEFGHIJ-DO-8987
First printing, April 1987

Contents

PREFACE *vii*

1. The Need *1*

2. Liberations *7*

3. The Shift *17*

4. Solitude *25*

5. Super-Abundance *35*

6. Survival *45*

7. The Self *53*

8. Action *61*

9. Courage *71*

10. Support *79*

11. Force *87*

12. Ease *99*

13. Everyday Courage *113*

14. The Return *135*

POSTSCRIPT *141*

Preface

ARE YOU COURAGEOUS? Do you need courage?
Your having opened this book implies that you have
some unanswered questions on the subject. And the simplest, most direct concerns your own level of courage.

Few would answer "Yes, I am" without feeling boastful.
More would say "No" halfway between humility and self-
denial. And most would feel confident with a "Sometimes,
but not often enough," which is probably the reason for
their interest in this topic.

Whatever your personal answer may be, there is some
good news coming: You deserve an unquestionable "Yes."
Yes, you are courageous, even though you doubt it, even
if you often meet with inner cowardice, even if you do not
know exactly what courage is all about.

You are courageous by the simple fact that you are a
human being living his or her own life. You simply could

not do that without access to courage, and several times a day.

But let us start with the more conventional view. Who exemplifies courage in this contemporary world? Patton, Truman, Iacocca, Sakharov? It is easy to agree on such names. The word "courage" is naturally associated with exceptional risks or deeds. This may be precisely why, for each of us living in a prosperous society, it seems to have slipped into disuse. Thank God such feats are not our everyday bread!

· Even if extraordinary feats are rare, courage abounds in everyday life, although often incognito. "No guts, no glory" is just a cliché and more than a little out of date. The truth of today sounds more like "No guts, no dignity, and even no identity." And who among us would feel whole without our dignity or a strong identity?

But what can we learn from the legendary heros? Well, more about the different levels of courage.

Whether they are real, like Bonaparte, Patton, or Sakharov, or fictitious like Achilles, Rambo, or the inevitable John Wayne, first come the heros. Their courage is indisputable as they risk their lives, and, often, lose them. Even if they fail to conquer they remain forever inspiring for having willingly pitted themselves against death.

Inspiring, but not necessarily appealing to the common person for whom risking one's life is low on the list of priorities. But if worst comes to worst, their example could prove handy.

Closer to us in experience and time are the tough: Truman on the eve of Hiroshima, Thatcher waging war with

Argentina, Reagan dismissing the air traffic controllers, or Iacocca taking the helm of a nearly bankrupt Chrysler Corporation.

The tough are not heroic since they rarely risk their lives, but dramatic because their decisions shape the destiny of others as well as their own. They know what is at stake for them personally—their place in history, reputation, or social standing—and they proceed with their eyes opened.

We all meet with such challenges in the business of living. They may not be as grandiose, but for us they often are as fateful. Going through a divorce, quitting a job, or selling one's home or business may be statistically banal situations, but when we have to face them we know we are confronted with destiny. Torn between courage and cowardice, we may also simply end up procrastinating.

The hope is that we don't have to use toughness as often as we use toothpaste, even if we can't sometimes escape it. Yet the necessity for courage is much more common, if not as intense, in ordinary situations than most of us think. Here is the more common use of courage, the courage for you and me . . . and Woody Allen. Undergoing a minor operation, staying home to work when the others leave for a party, setting the alarm clock for a four-hour night's sleep, not opening the cookie jar. Everyday courage.

This kind of small-change courage is neither heroic nor dramatic, but it defines, more than the "higher" ones, our personality. Each of its usages determines an attitude. Each of these attitudes draws one of the lines that make up the image of our self. This is "existential courage" because it is intertwined with what living is all about.

"Existential," when we take upon ourselves the consequences of being born, but also, quite simply, when we function as a person.

This is why, in a way, speaking of a "return of courage" makes no more sense than announcing the return of oxygen. It is always here, and always has been, universally. Nobody can do without it.

We can, however, call it a return in two ways. First, to the extent that courage had almost become a forgotten word in the descriptions of human behaviors. It was too emotional, too vague, too moralistic for the psychologists and the analysts. Just as were the words "will" or "effort." Simply put, we did not dare to use it in the recent past for fear of ridicule.

Second, we can speak of the return of the awareness for the necessity of courage in the face of an increasingly difficult world. The average American, after more than ten years of a stagnating standard of living, rising unemployment, and increasing worldwide competition, clearly perceives that more than education and good health is needed in order to survive. If courage were listed on the commodities market, its value would have risen greatly since the beginning of the eighties.

Is there, however, something specifically American about courage, or specifically courageous about Americans? As a European observer, crossing the Atlantic several times a year for the last thirty years, I have inevitably mused about that question.

If Europe, from ancient Greece to Rousseau, has been the bedrock of individualism, America may be seen as its practice ground. The pilgrim, the cowboy, the candidate, the entrepreneur, and even the gangster and the corporate raider are in our eyes as American as jeans and Coca-Cola. In French, there is no translation for "self-made man." We use the American word because it is an American concept, an American product. And no man can "make" himself without vast reserves of courage.

But even being American does not necessarily mean being courageous. Proof is in the massive cancellations by American tourists and celebrities of trips to Europe when some bombs exploded in Paris. The rest of the world still came.

America is also, for we Europeans, the country where kids are overpampered, little old ladies are obsessed with germs, and where few people can resist junk-food diets.

One can also think of a good number of places in the world where it takes much more courage to live than in America (or Western Europe). For instance . . . just about everywhere else.

But if there is such a thing as an American character, then the notion of risk is part of its very fiber, despite the existence in the U.S. of mammoth insurance companies and herds of lawyers. "Making it," "climbing the ladder," "surviving" belong to the contemporary set of American values, and they do indeed rhyme with courage.

Europeans used to scorn the American social system which gives so little protection to the salaried worker. Complete social security, high severance pay, long maternity leaves, and six weeks a year vacation are all now part of the European way of life.

We used to think that, because the Americans did not enjoy the same benefits as we did, they were behind the times and would have to catch up. But during the last five years the mood in Europe has changed. Today Americans appear less burdened, more adaptive, apt to take more risks. They are in greater accord with today's global economic conditions than we Europeans.

The result of these differences in attitudes and practice can be measured. Over the last ten years, the standard of living has kept pace, making progress in Europe, but not in the U.S. But unemployment has declined in America, not in Europe. More comfort in Europe versus more courage in America?

The new generation of Americans is facing a greater challenge. On the one hand, the global readjustment of business has compelled them to return to a work ethic that closely resembles that of the 1950s. On the other hand, they cannot forget the legacy of the 1960s and its promise of fulfillment. This paradox was perfectly stated on the label I once read inside an Oshkosh garment: "For hard work and easy living."

Combining these two requires even more personal choices, commitments, and responsibilities. It was easy in the past to conform, that is, to follow all of the rules that you chose once and for all. But today, conformism is almost a technical impossibility, since none of the diverse life-styles and models in America is dominant. There is no mainstream value system to conform to anymore.

This coincides, in advanced countries, with a weakening of most of the traditional support systems: churches, unions, and political parties. There are many good aspects to these trends: more freedom, fewer constraints, more options, and more responsibilities. But also, more risks and more isolation.

This is what explains, and at the same time calls for, a return of courage. Not heroic courage, and rarely tough courage, but the one with which each individual chooses his or her path in a complex, difficult, but at the same time interesting and promising environment. Everyday courage in search of happiness.

What Europeans and Americans have in common, along with prosperity, is a new maturity, which helps them acknowledge the fact that no longer, and now less than ever, can they define themselves through their links to a country, a corporation, even a family. It may lead us to long for the time when we could, but it nevertheless coincides with today's realities.

Most of what conditions one's own life is, and will more and more be, decided and acted upon freely by each of us. For Europeans more attuned to the ideologies of the solidarities and mass movements of the last century, it is a shaking rediscovery. For Americans who have been told early in their video education that, when in trouble, one can always "bite the bullet" or "hit the trail," it may only be a reminder.

As a child in Paris, on my way to school I would pass by the statue of Benjamin Franklin, sitting forever on the side of the Trocadero.

A statue to inspired common sense and to the go-between who made old France and new America lifelong friends. To the earlier question, Is there something American about courage?, maybe Benjamin Franklin can provide an answer.

The France he came to was the land of aristocratic courage: military, with Turenne and Condé; political, with Richelieu; or literary, with Voltaire. In such a kingdom it took, however, a much greater courage to be a peasant and endure the incredible hardships of a still primitive life. But this was not acknowledged until after a revolution had been fought.

Franklin, by his appeal to both the efforts and the freedom of the common man laboring in his own destiny, legitimized peasant courage. He helped promote the awareness that through everyday courage everyone had the opportunity and the right to become a citizen. Along with the ambitious ideologies that shaped modern times, there was a need for this tool of the spirit.

In old regime Europe, courage was recognized only as a noble virtue, the people had to resort to fortitude. Americans like Benjamin Franklin helped change that perspective and, in a way, they democratized courage.

America's contribution to courage may have been, historically, this recognition of its presence and value in every individual. Where it belongs.

THE *Return*
OF *Courage*

1. *The Need*

THERE ARE ONLY TWO important kinds of courage: the courage to die and the courage to get up in the morning. All other courage stems from these or is inspired by them. But, with or without courage, we cannot avoid facing either death or a new day. They are moments from which there is no escape. So why do we need courage? What difference does it make, since these two events are in fact unavoidable?

Death awaits the condemned, both he who is dragged, trembling and sobbing, to the scaffold, and he who patriotically proclaims, "Give me Liberty, or give me Death!" It was not in dying that Nathan Hale displayed great courage, it was in choosing to face up to it, to exist fully to the very end. The difference may seem slight, but it is crucial. Nathan Hale lived the last minute of his life *better*.

Courage allows us to live better, not only our last minute better, but even more important, every minute and day that went before. Courage plays a part in everything we do, even when we aren't aware of it.

There are cases where the absence of courage makes all the difference. Raoul Dautry, a member of the Cabinet of the Third French Republic, told how, one day in 1938, when he was in Germany for the dedication of a new dam, he found himself standing behind Adolf Hitler on the edge of a hundred-and-fifty-foot-high concrete wall. "Shall I push him over?" he asked himself. But he didn't have the nerve. Of course, he would have been shot down by storm-troopers, but his death would probably have forestalled millions of others. Who, though, can reproach him for failing to act? None of us can swear that, in his place, we would have had the immediate courage to shove the Führer into the void.

A more commonplace incident: I am riding a train when I see a woman who attracts me. I want to talk with her, but my nerve fails me. A few moments later, she gets out and the chance is gone. No courage, nothing happens.

We could say that courage has two different aspects. When we are faced with the inevitable, such as when we confront death, it determines our attitude; when we confront daily uncertainty, it conditions the outcome. But are these two aspects of courage so different? We can only speak of courage when in situations where we can make a choice. But, like Nathan Hale, even facing death we still have a choice, our way of facing it.

All that follows in this book will confirm that we cannot take action without courage. And since we are constantly moving from one action to another without any awareness that we are especially endowed with courage, then, plainly, courage can be there without our being aware of it.

When I get up in the morning after only three hours sleep, it demands a bit—however small—of courage. But if it is in order to start on an exciting trip, I get myself into the bathroom without much trouble. It took some small piece of courage to overcome being tired, but my high motivation, much more powerful, made me unaware of it.

Traditionally, courage has been seen as a moral or spiritual virtue, often with military connotations. This was the courage celebrated by the ancient Greeks, typified by Achilles. Later our civilization had the Captains Courageous, facing a storm at sea; Joan of Arc climbing the ramparts of Orléans; John Wayne in *The Alamo* falling, outnumbered, while firing his last round. All folklore of the past, which has played a part in relegating courage to the shelf of spare parts, no longer in demand. . . .

But the courage of which we have daily need has little to do with the courage of Joan of Arc. Without either special merit or vainglory, *it's a matter of leading my life in the best possible way, even when there is no witness but myself.* So it is not a moralizing kind of courage I need, it is a psychological wellspring, necessary to my existence.

Just lately, after her son had committed suicide, one of my friends found the note he had left behind. "Mother, you didn't tell me that it takes courage to live." All of our generation have cherished the hope that progress, prosperity, technology, a more just and better organized world, would make courage—which we instinctively couple with trials, tribulations, and fatality—a virtue of times gone by.

And not unreasonably. The great wars were far behind

us. The last battlements of Victorian ethics had been dynamited by protesting students in the 1960s. Education floundered in a psychoanalytical soup, presenting the individual as the end-product of his instincts and his unconscious. If anyone was at fault it was our parents, or society.

In trying to forget centuries of poverty and constraints, we thought we had no more need of old-fashioned virtues such as will, effort, discipline, and courage.

Psychologists, therapists, and teachers hardly dared to pronounce any of these words unless they be taken for old-fashioned fools. And not illogically. The hope that a revolution would better everything at once was a constant of our times. The spread of the gospel according to Freud, antibiotics, and supermarkets led us to hope for uncomplicated happiness. The "Death of History," and its painful reminders of our past, was even spoken of, as if we could do without a past.

But times, and our mood, changed again. The economic recessions of the 1970s don't explain it all. In fact, the ninety percent of the population not unemployed suffered only a slight decline in its personal income. But it was enough to signal that progress had come to an end.

Only five years elapsed between the naive slogan "Anything Goes" and the shock of the oil crisis. There were brutal disappointments. The system didn't work. Economists were running out of answers. The bureaucracy of government did not respond to change, and our future seemed uncertain. The dogma of our century, that social remedies ensure us protection from uncertainty and bad luck, began to waver. On the heels of our new idealism came an old saying, "Heaven helps those who help themselves." Our economic woes have led to another and deeper, although implicit, conclusion. *Progress hasn't altered Man's fate, the human condition.*

Modern life puts us up against some of the same problems as those Shakespeare faced. And so we now seek out and dust off the lifejacket we had so hastily thrown away; once more we take an interest in will, effort, and courage.

Many of the ideas voiced here may seem as old as the world, which indeed they are. But although humanity's problems are not new, each one of us has to face them for the first time in our own lives. Every generation in its turn passes through the labyrinth.

From *The Song of Roland* to *For Whom the Bell Tolls* we have referred to the same kind of courage. The last man of the rear guard holds the pass and gives up his life for his comrades, whether blowing Roland's horn or wielding a machine gun. Those heroes, though, are dead. The courage that interests us here is not a springboard to posthumous glory; it is a force that keeps us in one piece, that prevents us from breaking up amid the vicissitudes of daily life.

The modern warrior—you and me—is a strategist throughout the course of his life; a tactician throughout his days. He defends, above all, his inner cohesion and logic. Gone are the mad charges, the clash of battlelines, so murderous, yet so simple to play out. The new hand-to-hand combat, whose battleground is within the individual, is all the fiercer in that it is complex and without retreat.

If courage has once more become indispensable, it is because no one else can win this battle for me, no one can fight in my place.

Faced with a solitude by no means new, but which more

and more shows itself, I have only everyday courage, often subtle, only occasionally more demanding. It is not along the line of "In case of accident, break glass," but, rather, like "Apply several times daily, as needed." It is courage as a style, as an ecological principle, to help me feel more free, more whole, even if I am all alone. Sometimes a single capsule, sometimes the entire box.

The course of life is long and challenging. If we examine it closely we see everywhere examples of courage. Finding ways in which to cope, to remain unscathed, occupy us all. But I have a dawning suspicion that protection is to be found in courage rather than in life insurance. The reasons, however, may not be obvious to everyone, and that is why the matter deserves sharper examination.

2. *Liberations*

W HAT COMPLAINT HAVE WE AS we approach
the century's end? Don't those of us lucky enough to
be born in Europe and North America live in a sort of
rediscovered paradise? Milk and honey flow in various fla-
vors under various trademarks. Peace reigns in our coun-
tryside; our bodies are healthy. We can move about as we
like and often travel great distances. Our entertainment is
delivered directly to our living rooms.

*Isn't modern man ungrateful in his complaint, in his dissat-
isfaction with the present, his pessimism about the future? What
are we missing?*

For centuries gone by our parents and ancestors waited
or searched for peace, justice, and prosperity. They are ours,
it may be said, and we are still dissatisfied.

I've never understood questions like: "At what period of
history would you have preferred to live?" When I consider

all that I've escaped there can only be one answer: my own. Like those who went before me, I had not four but eight horsemen of misfortune at my heels. Only now, they are giving signs of exhaustion. Four of them—poverty, disease, oppression, and war—were after my body. Four others—ignorance, religion, moralism, and ideology—were after my mind.

POVERTY

Poverty has not disappeared altogether (it exists, without question, even in our society), but it has become marginal. Its decline is relatively new. At the beginning of the nineteenth century, most of our population had a standard of living not very different from that of their feudal ancestors. As recently as this century the average person could count on but a fraction of the material wealth we rely on today. Not only do unemployed people no longer starve to death, even in the face of our ongoing economic "crises," consumption continues to increase, if a bit more slowly.

DISEASE

Until early in the present century a woman had to bear six children in order to have three survive; the others died very young. Before the Second World War, our life expectancy was fifty years; today it is over seventy-five. Cancer may have become an obsession, but we no longer die of infectious diseases such as tuberculosis, diphtheria, or pneumonia. Medicine may not yet give us our money's worth, but it is everywhere available. We even hear that, in many areas, there are too many doctors.

OPPRESSION

As I butter my toast, there are in the world people who are besieged for their religious beliefs, sent to insane asylums for their political opinions, segregated by law for the color of their skin, deported for their nationality, stoned for their sexual preference, and executed for things which Western law does not even consider crimes.

Certainly the powerful enjoy privileges; there are rapist policemen, paranoid little judges, a host of lying politicians. But there are also newspapers to expose them and laws to defend us. We are so accustomed to freedom that we tend to forget that democracy could barely stammer two hundred years ago and that, over the whole planet, it is still a minority form of government.

WAR

What if war were really outmoded without our knowing it? It will be a long time before we can be sure, perhaps a hundred years. But our attitudes about war have changed. In times past, every generation expected to experience a war, and rarely was it disappointed. My father lived through two, and not the smallest. Since, there have been regional conflicts, a dose of Koreas and Vietnams, but for forty years there has been no conflict on European soil nor on a global scale, and none ever in America that was not tragically self-wrought.

Fear of nuclear catastrophe plays a decisive role. The threat broods over us, mad sums are spent on armaments, but we are still at peace. The human race may be on the brink of annihilation but meanwhile we die in our beds, and it isn't at all obvious that Nuclear Armageddon is inevitable.

If, within fifty or a hundred years, we are not charred by the bomb or frozen by the nuclear winter to follow, it is because, on August 6, 1945, sixty thousand Japanese dead made war unthinkable. An important first in our history. Uncertainty lies ahead, but our chances for a century of peace cannot be disregarded.

IGNORANCE

About the essential questions we shall probably always remain ignorant, and we have no choice but to rely on our intuition for answers.

The lack of access to a basic education has always been a reason for dependency, exploitation, and oppression. As long as one had to be a nobleman or a priest in order to be educated, democracy had little chance of enduring.

After one educated elite had succumbed to the forces of revolution, another, almost identically structured, soon took its place. More than a century had to pass before Horace Mann disseminated the seeds of mass education and made it a pathway to power.

But the seeds of learning do not sprout overnight. In 1900, one high school graduate out of a thousand went on to higher education; in 1955, one out of ten. Today, one out of three gets an advanced degree. This is a mixed blessing. The value of a college education has lessened, and no longer does it ensure the success it once did. But whatever the economic benefits, the importance of access to education is widely recognized.

RELIGION

For twenty thousand years religion has occupied a central place in our culture. It has three distinct forms: church, doctrine, and spirituality. The first two, exterior by nature, vary according to time and place. Their purposes should only be to satisfy the spiritual needs of human beings confronted by their fate. But, in all organized societies, they have tended to occupy the entire scene, eclipsing and evicting spirituality.

The Church is a power structure with all the compromises that this entails. With the passage of time, the doctrine of any religion becomes or is felt to be a constricting mass of precepts. It should not surprise us that, in contact with a technological civilization, this ready-made structure should crack. Dogmas are static by definition, and today everything is in flux. We had to reduce the power of the Church and combat the influence of doctrines in order to develop into autonomous individuals.

In our haste, however, we have thrown out the spiritual along with the holy water, thereby creating an apparent void.

Nevertheless, the recently achieved secularization of political systems and life-styles marks an important stage in the liberation of modern man.

MORALITY

Doctrines impress themselves deeply on men's minds; that is why they continue to hold sway long after religious practices have crumbled. Even atheists still recognize our culture as "Judeo-Christian" and measure their ethics by the Ten Commandments.

It is easier to convert a church to condominiums than to change our moral principles.

Hence the more—than—symbolic importance of the passing, less than a generation ago, of sexual taboos with their baggage of convention, hypocrisy, and repression, not to mention an inexhaustible store of guilt.

Our emancipation in this respect is too recent and incomplete to allow the establishment of a new psychological and social balance, and by no means are we all at the same stage. But we cannot but feel that we have here the beginning of a reconciliation between the individual and his self, of another conquest to be credited to the last years of the twentieth century.

IDEOLOGIES

Religion not only regulated the social structure (if you don't strike it rich in this world, you'll get your reward in the hereafter); it also gave a seal of legitimacy and endurance to the political structures intertwined with its own. Its influence was as worldly as it was spiritual, as political and social as it was individual.

In order not to pull down the wall when stripping off the ivy, the nineteenth and twentieth centuries invented a replacement known as ideology, a sort of secular religion in which Man had taken over the role of God. Deprived of a central figure to worship, believers are exhorted to show stricter respect for texts and doctrines.

Hence the ferocity of the various kinds of fascism, communism, and other exotic personality cults which have none of the flexibility and indulgence that the Church had acquired in the ten or twenty centuries of its existence.

Although, because of the enormity of their crimes and the rigidity of their economic set-up, these political systems have already lost much of their appeal, they stay afloat by means of a police network based on informers and strict control of information.

It is only recently that Marxist-Leninism, the most ambitious (and, over the years, the most murderous) of these ideologies, has lost its hold on the intellectual elite of the Western World. In the mid-1970s the blast of the white tornado, Solzhenitsyn, cleared the last remnants of communist intellectuals from an active role in Western society. This time, God is really dead.

When I cast a glance in the rear-view mirror and see the eight horsemen of misfortune falling down and even dying at the edge of the road behind me, I am glad that I was not born in any earlier age. I would have had to struggle, then, against those forces of the past that still tyrannize over most of our Third World and communist contemporaries. Here, in the West, their comparative eclipse allows us to climb further toward the summit of our true destiny.

This succession of liberations is miraculous and, at the same time, limited. For from what have the billion or so privileged persons—among whom both the writer and the reader of this book—liberated themselves? Only from a long, primitive phase of history from which we are barely emerging and where others still grope.

Physically, materially, and politically we are coming out of the Middle Ages. But the essential has yet to be accomplished, since on psychological, affective, and spiritual levels we are still immersed in them.

Sisyphus, whom Camus called upon forty years ago, is

still condemned to push his great stone up the hill, eternally to have it slip from him and roll down again.

But he incarnates contemporary courage, the kind we need when we realize that the task is never done, that it simply changes level. Even this change is, in itself, passionately interesting.

Camus published his *Myth of Sisyphus* in 1942 during the last "just" war. Good was going to crush Evil (the Middle Ages again), after which the courage of revolutionary man (from Mao to Guevera) would give a new face to an old, simplistic myth. The Final Struggle or the Long March, on the way to singing tomorrows: a simple remake of Saint Bernard preaching the First Crusade. These were the revolutionary phantoms that haunted our early youth, sent us forth to do battle.

Now, however, there's no use in trying to send troops to the attack with the slogan, "Get yourself killed in order that the survivors may attain new and even more complicated pains-in-the-ass!"

Our malaise stems from the fact that the more we know, the less innocent we feel. And even the young feel the same way, maybe all for the better. The mythical Sisyphus has finally turned out to be more real than Patton, Guevera, or the Chicago Seven, whose stories had seemed to us more edifying, agreeable, or amusing to hear.

And so, what is our complaint as we near the end of the century? Simply our realization that, after achieving many of the dreams of the philosophers of the eighteenth century, the scientists of the nineteenth, and the revolutionaries of the twentieth, the Difficulty of Being is still there.

Come Sisyphus, back on the road! If our rock had fallen

back to the bottom of the cliff there would be reason for despair. But we rest on a plateau. The slope ahead may be steeper than the last, but at least it's new. With our innocence and illusions lost we see the possibilities of new explorations. What could be more interesting?

Courage!

3. *The Shift*

THE BRAVE LITTLE SOLDIERS of progress have won their objectives, but they haven't found happiness. They have no new goal to pursue, and they are depressed.

There are two different explanations for this current discomfort, both equally valid. Superficially, we lack memory, inspiration, and a sense of proportion. More profoundly, we are probably approaching a new stage of human consciousness.

Our memory isn't that good anyway, but the modern media have conspicuously shortened it. In the cottages of old, watching by the fireside, the elderly told their stories and the middle-aged spoke of the little they knew, learned from experience. The extent of their knowledge was narrow, but it was deeply rooted in the past.

Today reality comes from the tube, which lays it out,

comments on it, and thinks about it on our behalf. The news of the moment prevails; references and comparisons to the past go no further back than the day, the month, or, at most, the year before.

Every single day, thousands of facts, figures, and images overwhelm our attention. Except for trivia and nostalgic flashbacks, we scarcely know how life used to be ten or twenty years ago.

The comparisons we make are based on percentages, in a manner both abstract and deceptive. In order to resharpen public interest continuously, the media must make the most of the smallest event. People, things, and values are quoted on the Stock Exchange of polls and samplings of public opinion. Our sense of proportion soon disconnects us from reality.

We grasp that the average purchasing power has gone down by one percent in the current year, but we no longer realize that, at all levels, we are three times as rich as our parents. Or that to live like a Czech, an Argentinian, or a Korean (not to mention an inhabitant of the Third World) is something we could not endure.

Our shortened rear and side visions enclose us in an arena of boredom, simply because the pace of social change has presently slackened, and no perspectives open up before us.

What is it that inspires or revives the morale of a community? Nowadays conquest by war is out. Kennedy inspired the conquest of the moon, a stimulating sight until it became as routine as the football season. What is there left for us to long for here and now? A new television network? . . . how exciting!

True leaders are scarce. Since ideologies are old-hat and economic panaceas have lost their credibility, our candidates for office have an applause meter attached to their belts. When the level drops, we discard them. If opera stars were treated the same way, they'd soon give up singing.

As for drama, there's nothing like the end of a war to inspire the thought "it feels so good when it's over." But our wars ended years ago, and now we're left with only the occasional taking of hostages to provide us with a thrill when they're freed. The media do all they can to give a worldwide resonance to these local vicissitudes, spun out like a mini-series over two or three days. But the repetition of such events has made them stale. No news-of-the-day holds us for long.

In contemporary society there are two real threats (aside from a nuclear apocalypse): unemployment and cancer. And in either case, we are promised no more than the hope of some improvement in the next century.

In short, the best the future has to offer seems to be *no more of the same*. We have come to the end of great collective projects and of ideological battles. And the lures with which society seeks to dazzle us have no more thrill.

We are now inheriting, each one of us, the legacy of our tomorrows.

It's not a matter of impasse; rather it's a shift, a passing of the baton, from the group to the individual. What collectivity could do for the individual is practically completed, allowing us to discern more clearly what remains for us to do.

Three disappointments goad the individual. In spite of

democracy he does not feel free, in spite of prosperity he is not satisfied, in spite of the relaxation of the moral code, the pain of living increases.

The entrepreneurial revival has more than just a business perspective. If people are attracted to it, isn't it because they feel personally that the next stage is theirs, that beyond a point which we are beginning to see, collective solutions have little more to offer?

To say this is not to label as mistaken the national and social preoccupations which have been paramount throughout the century. On the contrary, it is because the eight horsemen we discussed above have been dealt with that each one of us sees the way clear before himself.

The gradual but steady tipping of the scales in favor of the individual marks an important moment in human history, one which will doubtless fascinate the great historians of the future. It is a trend that is working itself out in the here and now, and if peace holds fast it will be irreversible.

And so we have the matter of courage in a new context. The individual to whom society is passing the torch of the future is aware that he will need more courage than ever before to make it on his own. Even more than he thinks because, as we shall see, other elements will arise to complicate his task.

What task?

The task of existing.

Being alive is the lot of every animal. As such we find ourselves thrown into life without having chosen it.

But as soon as we become aware of it, we are faced with the problem of our existence as a person; that is, the problem of our place in the world and of our life's meaning.

Beginning with the dawn of human consciousness men have been faced by "existential" questions, bound up, as the word implies, with our very existence. To take only the three most burning ones:

· What am I doing here?
· What is good and what is bad?
· After death, what?

Unfailingly, these questions are the source of our anxiety. In order to live, function, and enjoy well-being, to be truly happy, perhaps, we must loosen the vise by finding some answers.

From time immemorial our forebears embraced two solutions: constraint and religion. One of the two would have been enough, but it was thought prudent to combine them.

Constraint may be summed up by Edith Piaf's song: "I'm far too busy to dream." For it is a mistake to interpret the biblical verse, "In the sweat of thy face shalt thou eat bread" as a curse. On the contrary, it is a blessing. If Adam and Eve had had nothing to do, they no doubt would have suffered from anxiety and fallen into depression, wondering all day long why they were going to die.

As long as food, clothing, heat, and self-defense were totally demanding, life had a full meaning. With a little luck a man died without self-questioning.

And if questions did arrive, religion supplied answers to the three we specified above, as well as to many others, often before there was the intelligence, or impudence, to put them into words. For from childhood on, one was indoctrinated.

Man's religious creativity dates farther back than even his technical virtuosity.

We can get along better without a watch or even a job than without a shield against metaphysical anxiety.

We solve the trials of our physical world far better than we face the problem of our individual existence. The system which flourished for thousands of years was to depend, alternately, on constraint and religion, neither of which, alone, could guarantee peace of mind. In the course of history we find individuals like Don Juan, who did without either. They were "strong-minded," able to face up both to anxiety and to society's criticism of their free and easy ways.

Now whole peoples have no religious answers and feel very little constrained.

If we had only to meet our essential needs, we could now work far less than we do. But in fact we don't. On the contrary, we often seem to be accelerating the pace. Otherwise, the floodgates of anxiety would open and find us with only outdated and vulnerable defenses.

The current dilemma, posed by many thinkers since the 1950s, may be summarized thus: the political and economic foundations of my liberation are at hand, but am I ready for it?

There has always been talk of Man's freedom, but only the members of a small, prosperous, and enlightened elite have had the opportunity to fully analyze its practical side. We live in a state of flux, because the material demands which glued our nose to the grindstone are loosening up and the social and moral structures which used to precondition us are fading away.

So here we are, free to be free, and it's a bit scary. Here is why study of the human condition of today must first bring up the matter of courage.

Not that we need it so much more today than yesterday. Every previous era has been marked by hardships whose memory still makes us tremble. Simply, it is the form that courage must take today that we must examine. This form stems from the analysis of the contemporary difficulty in modern life. And the fact that life is now easier than existence is at the heart of the problem.

This is no paradox. To exist as a free individual, in the face of infinity and death, such was and is the lot of those who lived before us and those who are at our side today. But few of us have had the time to have more than a glimpse of our condition.

We cannot shrink from our lucidity, but that does not mean it is easy to accept, nor that the conditions for doing it are ideally serene. But if we take this pretext to evade the unfolding development of our destiny, we lay ourselves open to blame, failing, in the only life we have, to use our full potential.

The vanguard of humankind is in the same plight as a young man who has to make up his mind to leave his parents' home. He is able to live independently, choose his values, take his own risks. And he is tempted to do so, because he can hardly bear the constraints otherwise imposed upon him. But he hangs back, for home, after all, is practical, comfortable, and free of charge.

That is where we are. Only natural to feel torn. It falls to us to find the courage to take the first step.

4. *Solitude*

WE ARE BORN AND DIE ALONE, that we all
know. But must we also live alone? Certainly today
more than yesterday, and this is probably for the best.

The situation of every human being, enclosed in his sack
of skin, is one of radical solitude. Even with close friends
or in a lover's embrace, communication with another is
only partial and transitory. This truth lends itself to the
most poignant appeals, to the greatest poetry. In it art finds
inspiration.

*But in rebelling against solitude we also deny the definition
of our self.*

If I exist as an individual, which is what I want, I can't
unite with anyone else without losing my uniqueness and
my autonomy. Plainly, I only "exist" alone. "Living" sets
forth other problems and evokes other, very varied responses.

We seem to bear our existential solitude better when living as a couple, a family, a group. But the price we pay is to be a little less ourselves in order to fit in with others. So great is the fear of solitude that most people find this price small and settle for it readily.

But the *self* does not so easily consent to being put down. And when it rebels, we witness all those misunderstandings, antagonisms, and painful ruptures which mark the history of our relationships. The *self* asserts its resistance by throwing us back into our solitude, like a boxer forced against the ropes.

Our age confronts us with our fundamental solitude in two domains, that of everyday life and that of our existence as individuals. If therefore I must take full responsibility for myself and leave my mark, it is obvious that no one else can do it for me.

An individual must realize and decide that he is not bound to an established group, doctrine, or system by himself. Many people never reach this stage of maturity, either because they have not had the benefit of favorable circumstances or because they have refused to face the implications of the simple fact of being alive.

For it takes courage to admit that I can escape neither my solitude nor my fear, even if actually being alone turns out to be less negative or painful than I had imagined.

Solitude can be fertile, captivating, exciting. But it is rarely sweet, for it includes a portent of death, which we all fear. And, in order to escape this fear, we are ready for all sorts of compromises and subterfuges, some of them even degrading.

Like death, solitude both terrifies and fascinates us. We

feel that it contains something unspeakable, and we wish we had the courage to approach it. But we can spend an entire lifetime in evasion refusing to explore and accept the depths, even the lowest depths, of our being, with all that they contain of both creativity and destruction.

This avoidance becomes impossible, however, once we take on the legacy of our culture and society and choose to be on our own. The solitude of the individual should not disconcert or hurt us. Since history now urges me to become the author of my own life, progress lies in refusing to give up control to anyone else, whether God or Caesar or Shrink.

Besides this philosophical solitude, which is anything but new, there is now, also, the contemporary, solitary life-style which increases our feeling of isolation.

How does society define one of its members? By his physical characteristics (height, weight, the color of his eyes), and by his social positioning, the business that employs him, the person to whom he is married, the city where he lives. It is almost impossible to identify me, in spite of the complexity of my personal make-up, except in terms of my physical characteristics and the groups to which I belong.

But group bonds have lost their strength. Those which have not disappeared have loosened their grip on us, as if the individual were casting off his mooring. Even the institutions we still think of as the most vigorous show signs of decline.

CHURCHES

Generally speaking, few of us still define ourselves by our religion. In Europe, only slightly more than one out of ten people, most beyond a certain age, attend religious services regularly. Only certain sacraments survive; "If it weren't for marriages and funerals, we'd never see the rest of the family."

Sunday church service once had a social function. People talked to one another as they came out of church; they had a chance to show off a new suit or dress and to invite friends to Sunday dinner. Nowadays there is no gathering place or rite that brings families and neighbors together. For something equivalent we must join a community or social group, and few people do so.

NATIONS

By sheer force of habit we still tell ethnic jokes and cheer for national teams. But the national image has faded considerably, even in the United States, and this is all to the good.

In Europe, what purpose is served by calling oneself French or Dutch when everywhere we drive the same cars, see the same American films, endure the same rates of unemployment?

There is talk of cultural identity. But the few people with sufficient culture to be identified by it are just the very ones who think internationally.

BUSINESS ENTERPRISES

Until recently, the workplace, whether private or government, substituted for the village square in providing meetings and exchanges. People spent the greater part of their time at work, and whether they stayed in one place for ten years or, as in Japan, for a lifetime, there came to be almost symbiotic bonds between the individual and his professional surroundings.

But both employers and employees, on the pretext of diversification or renewal, now prefer shorter-term contracts. And, with every new job, bonds have to be reknit. With this as the status quo, companionship among fellow workers is slow to turn into lasting friendship.

TRADE UNIONS

Union leaders everywhere are aware of falling membership, although they cannot fathom the reason. Aside from unemployment and a growing distaste for politicalization, there is an increasing resort to individual rather than collective action. There is a feeling, more instinctive than reasoned, that mass action has reached the limits of its effectiveness. Of this, the weakening of the unions is the most recent and tangible sign.

POLITICAL PARTIES

Now that, during electoral campaigns, candidates have to hire people to paste up posters instead of relying on the usual party volunteers, and meetings are held more often around a table than in a public square, it is plain that party loyalties belong to the past. Parties have given up ideologies (except for extremists, who are considered laughable for this very reason) and hardly dare publish a platform.

Why should a citizen involve himself when he sees that the most important problems are no longer determined by politics?

THE COUPLE

Now that convention, moral restraint, and legal bonds have been discredited, the bubble is quick to burst forty to fifty percent of the time. Our image of the couple has changed. It no more implies the ancient linkage of production and procreation intended to favor the man's professional development and a budding family. Now we have the chance meeting of two individuals, looking for happiness but impelled, in order to cope with the uncertainties of life, to keep their independence.

The very fact of having to reckon with the risk of the failure of their union introduces a centrifugal force into their relationship. Both partners are on the alert for the signs of a crack. They make much of problems which, in the preceding generation, would have been either solved or nipped in the bud, but never would have torn them apart.

Planned obsolescence seems to be built into the very notion of today's couple.

Other relationships may follow, but while they should obviate solitude, their very number often intensifies its impact on us. The end of the myth of eternal love is today's most powerful spur to awareness of our fundamental solitude.

THE FAMILY

If there is any life raft left this should be it. We change our lovers, employers, residences, and opinions, but parents and children remain the same. Even when everything else gives way there is still the biological bond, that is, until the spread of test-tube babies introduces further confusion. But the life raft has shrunk, and aboard it we often tear each other apart.

The family upon which we fall back has no connection with the tribal country family of days gone by. In Europe now as in America, we hardly know when and where our grandparents were born, we no longer visit our cousins, we live with one of our divorced parents and the children of his or her new spouse. Many adults are bound to their parents only by enlisting them as baby-sitters while they go off for a weekend and/or a whole vacation.

Even if parents do not divorce early on, the family's real existence is limited to the twenty to twenty-five years it takes to educate and launch the children. Then the parents find themselves practically alone with one another should they still live together, with a considerable period of life before them.

Add to all that has been said the anonymity of big-city life and we can measure the rapid atrophy of all the systems—large and small—which gave preceding generations a sense of belonging.

Moreover, the spread of graduate studies demanded by increasing specialization combines with the loss of traditional supports, to produce the most modern solitude of all: meritocracy.

Formerly affiliation with a class or clan compensated for the chance elements of birth and education. But now, unless we make a sudden advance in our adult years, the course of our life depends on the baggage we have accumulated before we are twenty-five.

Meritocracy is a worldwide phenomenon. Students are ferociously keen on getting into particular colleges, and more and more we read of parents who start to worry about their children's future success when they are still in the primary grades. Will it soon be that life can be a failure at age seven?

Inequalities still play an important part in the strategy and financing of education, handing out trumps to some children and handicaps to others. But whereas before the family or its influential friends could still provide an underequipped young person with a cushioned career, now advanced studies are what count. So much the worse for those who have not taken advantage of the chance their parents gave them to develop their brains!

Meritocracy, then, adds its weight to the swing of the scales from the collective to the individual. And economic difficulties lead governments to define more narrowly the limits of what social security, insurance, and welfare programs can guarantee to the citizen. But when we call up this financial aspect of the program we must not forget that it is only the outward sign of a deeper change of direction connected with the retreat of ideologies.

A single idea has dominated our century, supported by the two pillars of contemporary thought, the psychology of Freud and Marxist socialism; namely, that the individual does not bear the main responsibility for what he is and does.

For Freud and for his heirs and successors, by the time we reach the age of taking control of our own life it is already too late; the emotional trials of our earliest years have left us prematurely scarred. For socialists, the educational, political, and economic structures of society dominate and manipulate us; alone we are weak and defeated.

These two a priori conceptions of human experience turn

us into vulnerable, powerless individuals, wanting to be taken care of.

Although today these two notions seem outdated, this does not mean that they were of no use in the past. Not too many years ago the majority of people were poor and ignorant. Today's majority is assuredly not rich and sophisticated, but the level has risen to such an extent that most citizens can assume responsibilities for their own lives.

"Make it on your own!" the System will more and more frequently tell us. "You are quite big and old enough and, as for me, I've no longer the means to take care of you."

Such is the threefold solitude of modern man: existential, *because no body of ideas offers him the answers he cannot do without;* emotional, *in that the traditional supports have eroded; and* social, *now that the State's protective structures are crumbling.*

Some may mourn this state of affairs and view the future with discouragement, as the domain of the lonely crowd. But it is possible, as well, to see a long-awaited progress. The ideal of an individual who is self-reliant amid the group to which he chooses to belong has its roots in ancient Greece and was incarnated by men of the Renaissance. The fact that it is no longer limited to the happy few, but is becoming accessible to the many, is to the credit of this era of Western civilization.

It is not by chance that there is a phrase to describe this new situation: *to take charge of oneself.* A little tough, perhaps, like the course of a solitary navigator, but very tempting.

Before embarking, however, we must study the reefs that lie ahead and outfit ourselves to cope with them.

5. *Super-Abundance*

THE FUTURE HOLDS OUT ITS ARMS, but my appointment book is full. I have constantly to postpone our meeting, because this advanced society, which frees me from so many problems of the past and which should allow me my independence, does not work automatically. A detail that changes everything.

Here I am, ready for the great adventure, ready to grasp the historical chance offered to my generation. Ready, yes, but not available. Is it possible that I've exchanged the physical and material constraints of the past for another, more insidious constraint, of a psychological kind? More modern, to be sure, but equally devouring.

The Ping-Pong game between my freedom and my solitude interests me, but I haven't the time to play.

I have not simply inherited the achievements of our System; I am one of its creators and also a cog in the vast machine. If I want to go on harvesting its advantages, the machine must work. To make it work, I must pay attention to it. And as I busy myself in this way, I trap myself.

For more than a century now we have lost ourselves in the condemnation or defense of the word "capitalism." Today we see more clearly that the key element of its growth was not the economic opportunities and resources, or the rise of mechanization; it was the intensive exploitation of the human mind, yours and mine.

In fact, the word "capitalistic" has become outmoded. Today, both East and West, we belong to the same "productivist system," spread now all over the planet. And productivity is the urge to produce *More, Faster, and Cheaper* every year, unfailingly. It's sheer madness.

The amazing thing is that we actually get it done. The system creaks and stalls at intervals, but not so very often if we consider the ground we have covered. *Productivity* is the iron rule of our time, one which no tyrant could have imposed upon us, but which we have brought upon ourselves, driven by our strange thirst for progress.

Technology and innovation play an important role, but what we invest and continually reinvest in the process is time, mental concentration, nervous tension, and motivation. Yours and mine.

We pay for saving on production costs by narrowing our lives. We are constantly performing. We deal with more problems, we keep on inventing, we communicate at top speed, we change residences, jobs, and even professions. *We* are the chief tools of the productivist system. And even the best tool eventually wears out.

Our personal tyrant weighs little more than two pounds,

but sometimes seems too heavy to bear. It has contrived the whole thing: the complexities, the techniques, the extravagant goals, and the ways of attaining them. Obviously it is overpowering, oversized in relation to the physical and emotional capacities of the individual who serves as its envelope and tool. We may be proud of our cerebral cortex, but its *More, Faster and Cheaper!* is exhausting.

Because of our minds, many of us will remain on the outskirts of the magical land of self-fulfillment.

For in winning out over the old curses we have set up new obstacles in our path: stress, super-abundance, and unreality.

STRESS

The Romantics suffered from spleen; our century's affliction is stress. It is not surprising that almost all of us are stricken. A roster of its causes merges with our picture of today's urbane scene: changes and separation (breakups, moves from one house to another, new jobs, divorces), difficulties in communicating with others, solitude, everyday annoyances (traffic jams, engine troubles, angry words stemming from short tempers), noise, ugliness, and the accelerated rhythm of life.

Stress in itself is not a bad thing. It is the organism's psycho-physiological reaction to stimulation, the famous Adaptation Syndrome, first described by Hans Selye, who invented the current use of the word. A compliment and an accusation result in two different kinds of stress, one agreeable, the other disagreeable. One causes our cheeks to redden, the other, to pale. But both provoke reactions.

Not so long ago an animal or a man subjected to negative

stress could externalize his reaction. To cry out, fight, back or run away, made for quick re-establishment of his inner balance (from heartbeats to glandular secretions). Henri Laborit has shown that civilized man has no such recourse, because his response is inhibited.

If one bumped into d'Artagnan, even accidentally, he drew his sword. But if your boss says something disagreeable to you, you can't punch him in the nose. Yet Laborit tells us they produce equivalent nervous reactions which, unable to find outward expression, pile up and turn upon our bodily tissues. We even know that stress promotes the three main threats to our health: cardiovascular disease, cancer, and depression.

It is not by mere chance that the conventional image of a candidate for a heart attack, the famous "Type A," matches that of a businessman at the pinnacle of success, always on the go, hurrying, trying to do more and more, and usually several things at a time, meeting with resistance or hostility real or imaginary. This knight of productivity is a man of action who hears no warning voice inside him, who has no individual thermostat.

Which one of us does not behave, at intervals, in "Type A" fashion?

There is a constant factor at the base of this behavior, and that is *insecurity*. It may go back to starved childhood affections or else simply stem from the conditions of contemporary life, where everything moves, nothing seems lasting, and a man can count only on himself.

Stress is not without its advantages: an exciting life, no time to ask ourselves tough questions, tangible material results. It may even give us the impression that we exist.

But anyone in a position of responsibility, at whatever level, may find that repeated or prolonged stress impairs his functioning. Among executives, the symptoms are obvious: difficulty in delegating tasks, uncertainty in decision making, inability to know one's strengths and weaknesses, hypersensitivity to criticism, loss of coolheadedness, inability to listen, a scarcity of friends, and little enjoyment of leisure. As for taking care of inner self, forget it!

SUPER-ABUNDANCE

How beautiful did abundance seem in a time of scarcity! Prisoners in the *stalags* dreamed of elaborate restaurant meals. Women with wooden soles on their shoes fantasized about high-heeled pumps. We anxiously awaited the resupply of such basics as butter, chocolate, gasoline. Who could have thought, forty years ago, that one day we should hesitate in front of a display of eighteen brands of butter and forty varieties of chocolates? A liberated Tantalus, long tormented by the sight of abundance just beyond his reach, is led to the buffet table of the Club Med, and here a new stress awaits him: the dilemma of choice.

Nature is fertile and generous. It secretes millions of spermatazoa in order to fertilize a single egg; it is more sumptuously wasteful than the most spendthrift potentate. But that prodigality happens automatically, without reflection.

If the society that we have built flooded us with only products and services, we should get on very well; better, certainly, than if it didn't. But the dizzying "too much" extends to every domain: too many images, too many acquaintances, too many appeals, too much information, too many demands from our surroundings, too many petty problems.

We have constantly to decide, without taking the time to be properly informed, to reflect on the relative importance of our decisions and, above all, on their consequences.

In fact, we should properly speak not of decisions but of *gambles* in regard to our professional, family, and financial affairs, where our reputation, our health, and our future are at stake. Often, because we have to rush from one thing to another, we sometimes don't even notice, much less analyze, the results of our decisions.

An excess of information, the bombardment of shorter and shorter messages, have conspicuously reduced our time for concentration. We are acquainted with an enormous number of things, but have the justified feeling that we don't really *know* or understand them. Another disturbing reason for insecurity.

The time has gone when, for lack of riches, we could lean on our knowledge. Faced by the multiplication of new discoveries and advances, with which we cannot keep up even in our own fields, we have a sensation of growing ignorance and see our own obsolescence on the horizon.

At the moment when we ought to be ready to face the world in a bold new way, our supports have collapsed and we perceive reality as more and more complex, multiplex. Small wonder that we feel dizzy.

UNREALITY

The result of the acceleration and proliferation of which we have just spoken is that, like a Hovercraft, raised by sheer speed above the waves, we have taken off from reality.

Three elements of contemporary life—comfort, money, and the media—have, without our awareness, woven a screen between us and reality.

For centuries man strove to protect his body from the rawness of the elements. But only recently have protective shields become available to the mass of the population. When private homes are overheated in the winter and air-conditioned offices cause us to shiver in mid-summer, then we have clearly left reality behind. The Montrealers who, in the dead of winter, drive in their shirtsleeves to an underground shopping center to buy strawberries have clearly evaded the reality of the seasons.

In a modern skyscraper, when we want to know the temperature outside, we turn on the radio, because sealed windows prevent us from sticking out our noses. Except for a few weeks of vacation every year, we go through life as through the transparent, intersecting tubes at Charles de Gaulle airport, from subways to elevators, from taxis to planes. We have foolishly placed the animal within us, which has its own need to exist, in a condition close to captivity.

Money has created an even deeper rift. At the beginning of the mercantile era, we made a considerable advance in paying for our food and clothing instead of having to produce them ourselves. When it comes to material goods, the act of purchasing makes for simplification.

But in our sophisticated society, money has taken on a mediatory role in far more subtle domains. We buy knowledge, relaxation, health, and security. The buying reflex causes us to acquire an encyclopedia for our instruction, medicines for the cure of our ills, and insurance for our protection. In this way we think we can short-circuit the interior transformation, the receptivity, that could make possible the effectiveness of these transactions.

We act—and sometimes even think—as if we could buy our lives, something that would be very convenient in view of the little time we have for living them.

Television, the latest and most spectacular of contemporary syndromes, divorces us from reality in two ways, by confusing our memory and distracting our attention.

The daily flood of images rolling over us is more varied, more rapid, more attention-catching than reality. They take over all the more easily in that our brain is already adept at creating images. Increasingly, it has become impossible to distinguish among the real, the imaginary, and what we have seen on the screen. Our personal lives are submerged by this collective pictorial invasion.

This form of media does more than saturate us with images; it also crowds our mind with pseudo-events. Television news throws into bold relief the items it reports by the mere fact of their selection. If a commentator enthuses over a certain sporting event or political election, he imposes his excitement upon the mass of viewers. We cannot choose our own subjects for meditation or amusement— that is, unless we turn off the TV and pick up a book.

We are intellectually and psychologically fed on a stream of indirect representations of reality which, in relation to the circumstances of our daily life, are pseudo-events. They do not really concern or affect us, but the power of their transmission gives them the upper hand and diminishes the validity of our own first-hand experience.

Our interior space has been invaded, and we have barely

taken notice. A fine scenario for a work of not-so-fictional science fiction!

An important example of our removal from reality is our lack of experience with tragedy. Violence, sorrow, and death are sublimated into innocuous images. Hence the preponderant place in our lives (and in the world of finance) of insurance and security systems.

We ward off tragedy in an attempt to make the real world like that of our childhood dreams; where nobody ever dies.

Dead bodies are not wanted; we are ashamed of them and keep them out of sight. Undertakers "restore lifelike color" so as not to wound the sensibilities of the survivors.

But since, quite evidently, tragedy has not gone away, far from it, and erupts when it pleases, its sudden appearance has a deeply disturbing and destabilizing effect. The invasion of horror or drama of any kind, and also of death, which comes later but is equally inevitable, finds us philosophically and psychologically unprepared.

Concurrent with the progress of the social security system there is an erosion of our spiritual security, in short, of our courage.

This overflowing, super-abundant world gorges and dizzies me. In its *More, Faster and Cheaper!* I am not at ease. The familiarity, the sense of belonging that underpinned my peace of mind, seems to be no more real than my childhood memories.

6. *Survival*

"Is there life *before* death?" is apparently the question in Prague, that capital of planetary depression. How can anyone be a Czech? Should we feel alive if, like the Czechs, we were squeezed between a petrified ideology and the interdiction of any individual initiative?

The question would be less witty, but more exact, if it ran: "Is there *existence* before death?" Living, breathing, eating, procreating, getting up and around in the morning, everyone does these things, in Prague as elsewhere. But existing—perceiving, understanding, expressing and developing oneself, choosing, creating, finding a meaning—these things are at a higher and obviously more desirable level. And which one of us can answer with a wholehearted *yes* the above question? *Metro-boulot-dodo,* as the French put it, subway—office—bed or stress—super—abundance-unreality. These make Czechs of us all.

In New York, the capital of stress but also of opulence, people have reached the point of talking about *survival*. In the concrete jungle, the rat race has resumed, after a slowdown to an only somewhat questionable jogger's pace during the 1970s. Just imagine! The richest, the freest, the most modern among us thinking in terms of survival!

Exaggeration thrives in New York; to be sure, not all of these paradoxes are without foundation. Are they making fun of us? In fact, survival can't be taken for granted by either the species or the individual.

The human species is up against only two crucial problems: to stave off shortages of food and energy and to refrain from blowing up the planet. The first requires management (of overpopulation, resources, and the substitution of one product or technique for another), and in this instance we do not lack the means of achievement. Here we should be able to attain a large measure of control. As for the risk of nuclear war, we have seen that it is not absurd to hope for a hundred years of peace and to proceed on the assumption that the world will not be annihilated.

For the individual, survival means, first of all, not to go from bad to worse. After escaping the dangers of centuries gone by, we must not succumb to the threats of the present day. The very factors that contributed to our liberation have left us as vulnerable as a baby emerging from an incubator. The structures that used to support as well as restrain us disappeared before we could forge any psychological armor in their place.

Our stores of will, serenity, optimism, and courage may seem somewhat inadequate in the face of the startling challenge we have evoked: to live alone and to live well as we face up to the world around us.

I tend to believe that these resources are likely to strengthen and increase over the next few generations, but meanwhile we have to live through a period in which our underdeveloped protective shell still leaves us vulnerable.

Our armor for survival will have to be courage, and we can see now where we shall use it. For, if existence implies that every one of us would have, at the very least, a place and a meaning, then these are two pillars we must defend. In the present state of the world and for perhaps a half-century to come, we now perceive more clearly that the complexity of the world makes it more difficult to define our place and keep it. Similarly, that our own facility and our alienation from ourselves confuses the very meaning of our lives.

COMPLEXITY

Since the realization that the future is no longer a synonym for progress, men have been moving forward on tiptoes. The triumphant advance of science and rationality had its crowning moment on July 20, 1969, with the fuzzy image of Armstrong's moon-boots bounding off lunar dust. There were grounds for cosmic pride in the accomplishment of one of man's oldest dreams. Since then, our dreams seem to be in trouble.

After sharing that historic vision of our planet, we have received nothing but bad news: a dirty war in Vietnam, young people turning their backs on society, a threatened scarcity of natural resources, a thousand tons of explosives for every inhabitant of the globe, oil in short supply, the Third World defaulting on its debts, whole peoples still starving to death; our own children faced with unemployment.

If the West, the economic Tarzan, is no longer able to manage its own business, then we lose face. There is gnawing worry: budgets are in the red, taxes could go up, we shall have to work longer hours to keep our living standards and our jobs.

Our surroundings, in the course of a few years, have not only become harsher, but seem undecipherable as well. A return to realism and modesty can do us no harm. It has finally been admitted that the almost automatic growth of the sixties could not extend indefinitely. Because we had not lived through the Crash of 1929 we lacked this wisdom. But we are beginning to acquire it.

The result is that we have reached the pinnacle of the economic-social pyramid. How can we establish a foothold?

Formerly we changed jobs in order to advance, like flat stones skipping over a lake. Now some dig holes and lie low, prepared for economic trench-warfare.

It's not a stampede but a concrete, worldly-wise version of every-man-for-himself-and-the-devil-take-the-hindmost.

This tougher competition doesn't necessarily entail the loss of our freedom of action. If, in my mind and in my actions, I need to take charge of myself as an individual, then it is a logical and natural thing to do the same on a social level.

In economics also, society has run out of big ideas. It is in the process of redefining itself, of thinking in terms of microcosms, the small unit of service or production, the individual. We can only be in favor of such a solution if for no other reason than that we have no alternative. But it will be an uphill climb.

When I feel energetic it is not too hard to keep my niche in a complex society, even if I have to cultivate some ambiguous qualities to do it, such as a certain tempered paranoia or tolerant cynicism.

But I am haunted by a sense of my own frailty. Moments of doubt multiply with diversity of choices. Out of the broad range of possible actions there emerges a fragmented self whose pieces I can't be sure will hold together. Once physical survival is no longer the great problem, worries shift to the inner front.

When ninety percent of the population was poor we were prey to hunger, filth, disease, ignorance, and fear. *Today's threats are depression, rejection, guilt, insecurity, impotence, boredom, absurdity, and—still and always—fear. We're no longer destitute, but we're anxious.*

Do we listen to ourselves too much? Yes, say the moralists: in time of war, mental institutions empty because more urgent matters claim attention. Perhaps so. But if, in order to calm our anxieties, we should have to return to poverty, then we may as well admit that human beings will never grow up.

The sharper our perceptions, the deeper our analyses, the better we penetrate the complexity and relativity of the business of life and the more we lose of our reassuring innocence. But, in compensation, we gain greater truth. Who ever said that truth is easy?

One of the specific frailties of the transitional generations to which we belong is the loss of the roots of feelings that are still within us.

Although I am free, independent, and disengaged from all systems, I am still not empty. I have values, principles, and reflexes which daily affect my behavior. As an inheritance of childhood, upbringing, and social osmosis, the Judeo-Christian moral code outlives the loss of faith. We are still programmed by beliefs that we have repudiated. In everyday life this gives us no trouble, but when it comes to certain fundamental choices, we realize that we no longer know on what basis to decide among them.

Our values are ad hoc, our ethics are day-to-day. No wonder that we lack courage; it is a plant that grows best out of rock.

ALIENATION

Certain Japanese executives say that they are not sure of living their own lives. I know others, closer by, who feel the same way. They live in part the life of their organization, in part the life of their family, in part that of Madonna. But what life have they of their own? The sum of these fragments? What can be worse than not to belong to oneself?

The abolition of slaves and serfs was the touchstone of recognition of the individual's integrity. What use is there in being finally liberated if I am not available to myself? Surely, no alienation could be deeper.

Production-minded society has succeeded in freeing us from a thousand constraints. In exchange, it asks for only one tribute: ourselves. Mephistopheles, here we come!

There's no need to wait for Hell in order to lose our souls. We can do it on the spot, everyday, by following a career that offers no perspectives, by soaking in information of no importance, by keeping up relationships devoid of feeling, by exchanging remarks empty of ideas, by attending performances without talent.

Existence depends on a genuine dialogue with ourselves. In order to perceive the constant flow of ideas, images, and reactions which go to make up our wealth and originality, we must have a minimum amount of leisure. Lacking time to ourselves and control of our lives, most of us are in contact with no more than two-fifths of our inner being. We hardly know ourselves, perhaps we don't want to.

Solitude holds no fears for those who bear themselves good company. If we haven't time to exist, to cultivate our inner resources, we are good company neither for ourselves nor for others.

A man who possesses serenity, character, and enough interests to beguile his solitude is able to attract and reassure others. He has no occasion to be alone, except for when he wisely decides to take time off for periodic renewal of acquaintance with himself.

There *is,* obviously, life before death, in Prague and else-where. But nowadays, it risks reducing itself to a pseudo-life, responsive only to external stimulation, dispersed in superficial contacts which give us only the illusion that we are not alone.

Our surroundings favor this state of affairs. Society, money, and sex games pose pseudo-problems to which it is fashionable to pay serious attention. Years can go by with-out a real look at how we live and who we are. Even the death of our friends is only slightly disturbing. Besides, why not just go on in this way? After all, it will soon be over. . . .

7. *The Self*

W<small>HAT IS IT THAT WANTS</small> not merely to live, but to exist?

Me, myself, would doubtless be our answer. At this point, then, it is imperative we better understand who this *self* is.

If I've written this book and you're reading it, it's because we both think that latching onto courage would help us to deal with the ordinary as well as the extraordinary circumstances of life. These circumstances, as they relate to our times, have, so far, been the objects of our examinations.

So here we are, up against them. You, for instance, whose eyes are following these lines and whose mind is extracting certain ideas from them, to be sorted out in the way that suits you best. Some of them seem to you to be on the right track, others of secondary importance, still others debatable or even wrong. This judgment is brought to bear by your *self,* that intimate, genuinely unique part of you, of which some portion will always remain undefinable.

To other people I am just another person, one of many interchangeable units. To nature I am a living being, a commonplace minor miracle, since I share this privilege with everything that isn't mineral. But as a human, I am the only animal that can think about himself and see himself as an object.

That which in this way looks into itself, which is conscious of being, which, by saying "I" takes on a name, is a self. And the self that I know best I call me.

It is not difficult to see the limits of the *self.* Others are not me, and vice versa. The material world outside my skin isn't me either. But when the *self* ventures to think of itself (Descartes understood that this was the indispensable premise of his existence) it gets into delicate philosophical problems.

To say "What is it in me that says *I*?" is not a tautology. The answer varies according to one's conviction. Christians would say that it is the soul, temporarily lodged in the body. Other, religiously minded people, that it is a part of the universal consciousness to which we belong, just as we do to the whole Cosmos. Materialists and Buddhists think that it is a system of perceptions produced and put together by the brain.

The acquisition of consciousness, the experience of the *self,* do not depend on personal convictions. They are common to us all. If our existence creates a problem, it's because the *self* isn't self-evident! As long as I'm alive it's always with me. Practically speaking we do feel it functioning as a center of perceptions and decision. It takes in information, handles it intelligently, and conducts the resulting actions, the exchanges of words and ideas with our material and human surroundings.

Is this enough to describe the experiences of the self, its *existence*? I put the question to *you* because each one of us must answer from inside that *self* which is his own true world, inaccessible to others.

Personally, I find that my *self* varies widely.

Sometimes it seems to me narrow and limited. Especially when a busy day causes me to pile one thing on another and to react ceaselessly to the questions and needs of others. This *self* works properly as a receiving and transmitting center, but it garners only passing impressions and sensations. The individual that others perceive as being Me has functioned efficiently. I alone know that in my essential *self,* I felt that day that I only fleetingly existed.

At other times, when circumstance (sleeplessness, a vacation, a long walk, a relaxed party or meeting, an occasion to be creative) makes me accessible to myself, this *self* unfolds, spreads out and blossoms. Intuitions, images, deductions open up like chambers and passageways before the searchlight of a cave explorer, and I feel as if, barring fatigue or an outside interruption, this state of mind could last indefinitely.

What about you?

The important part of life, the sensation of existing, can only be found at the level of the *self.*

Our biological and social sides should step in only to contribute and serve as tools to this essential feeling. The other way around, and our *self* is swallowed by physical necessities or social functions, we are not in a state of true "well-being."

There is much talk, in our day, of a return to individualism and narcissism. Rightly so, since the individual is taking his just place at the front of the stage. These attitudes converge with what interests us here: to reinforce the *self,* to ensure its scope, vigor, and opportunities to develop.

Fostering the affirmation of the self, *in times when many no longer clearly see* who *they are (even, occasionally, to the point of not knowing very well* if *they are), such is the implicit priority of this book.*

A good relationship with the *self* is, then, a condition of well-being (this is a tautology). But our very perception of the *self* is blurred by the noise (stress, disturbances, demands) of today's environment. Beyond this mere perception, the deepening of our self, the development of a dialogue with oneself, necessitates leisure, calm, and silence. In the absence of these, we cannot inhabit our solitude without anxiety.

To exist implies having full consciousness of the *self,* and enjoying it. But under today's conditions this is possible only at the price of a hard-fought battle to defend the *self* and win it more space.

In this battle the *self* cannot do without courage. I make my mark on myself and the world through the intermediary of action. And, in order to act, I *must* have courage.

The *self* is not as constantly present as life. Life is there from our first to our last second. There are only two possibilities, I am either alive or dead.

The *self,* on the other hand, builds itself up, fades out

(with every loss of awareness), and can be described in subtle quantitative and qualitative terms. Some people have a retiring self, others one that is cumbersome. In short, the *self* is changeable and unstable.

The minimum of self, the basis of every human's healthy mental life, lies in the essential distinction between self *and* non-self.

"Self is Me." Everything and everybody else, the entire Universe, belong to another category, the non-self. This distinction is not innate; it is only gradually acquired from the beginning of life on. After his birth, at first, a baby continues to think that his mother's body and his own are one. If we show his face in a mirror he doesn't understand that it belongs to him.

To understand and then to admit the dichotomy between *self* and *non-self* is fundamental, because it defines the individual in his own eyes. It is dramatic, as well, for it locates our solitude in regard to the rest of Creation. It is in early childhood, with the first separations, that this dichotomy appears. Its acceptance costs us intense interior torment, of which we find traces in the later phases of our existential uneasiness.

The very act of birth is the beginning. It is the parents who make birth into a joyful occasion; the arrival of the frail, innocent creature bearing their mingled genes fills them with delight. But the newborn, in his first cry, isn't fooled. He doesn't yet know that he'll have a *self,* but he seems to have grasped, at once, what Cioran calls "the inconvenience of being born."

He has been torn away forever from an almost perfect environment. Surrounded by the amniotic fluid of his mother's womb he was fully satisfied, without desires, worries, or clashes. And above all, with no barrier between himself and the rest of his Universe. In the actual fusion with another, his mother—an unforgettable experience which he will pathetically and vainly try to re-establish for the rest of his life—he was one with his environment. There was no feeling of being finite or alone.

After the embryo's third month there begins the cerebral activity that retains traces of the beatitude which Freud described as "oceanic," and that anchors in the unconscious an ideal standard of global well-being.

In comparison to this fetal period, everything else is bound to seem incomplete. And yet we keep only a vague uterine memory of these nine months, one that we cannot consciously call to mind.

Birth, then, is the first experience of an incurable separation, one which gives rise to the myths of paradise lost, the golden age, a fall from grace. It explains, also, our repeated attempts to rediscover, in love, friendship, worship, political activism, or even scuba diving, the fusion whose loss is a constant source of anxieties and desires. At the same time, the *self* is built up on this separation.

From the primal separation of birth to the final rupture of death, the existence of the self is strengthened by an uninterrupted succession of breakups, fractures, and differentiations.

After the estrangement of birth comes that of weaning. Then an absence of the mother is the first conscious wrench. After that, life's regular course; the school that takes us away from home, the friends that we make and lose, then the end of family life, often hastened by our parents' divorce, short-lived love affairs, changes of our home and workplace, the deaths of our friends, and, finally, the gradual weakening of our own body.

The *self* which comes out of each of these trials or passages is either fortified or impaired. We know that childhood separations, too brutal or unaccompanied by love, can inflict wounds whose devastating effects do not show up until later.

On the other hand, a *self* capable of facing up without too much fear to transitions and renouncements draws from them an inner serenity and a powerful stimulus spurring the individual to act upon the outside world.

Intra-uterine life before the experience of separation gives us an implicit and unforgettable reference to our unity with the world. This peace, this total absence of desires (desires which will arise only later on, together with the experience of lacking), are at the base of our projections of immortality and the infinite, and hence of our spirituality.

This unrestricted womb-like life also establishes in the body our innate taste for self-sufficiency and omnipotence. If this feeling is not too damaged by the trauma of our early years, it makes for a basis of self-confidence on which to build our personality.

Soon after birth the experience of needs (food, warmth, caresses) and then of desires makes us understand that satisfaction is not part of our own personal system but depends on exterior sources. Thus, the distinction between the *self* and others takes shape in practice. At the same time, a repeated experience of frustration is born of the realization that others do not always or immediately accede to our will.

In this way the two poles—union and separation—between which the *self* oscillates in the course of its existence, are formed. Separation makes for individuality and independence, but calls for solitude and courage. Union approaches, but does not attain, the original peace of which we have spoken; its price is dependence on others and having to be content with an incomplete paradise.

It is in knowledge of these two poles and the admission that we cannot attach ourselves permanently to either—because the dance of life goes on between them—that we find the road to our maturity.

To accept our dependence makes us more human; to free ourselves from it, even temporarily, is a source of strength.

We should lean on these alternatives in order to manage ourselves with psychological efficiency. The individual, at times a natural and social animal, at others solitary and creative, ends up by putting a veritable technology of the *self* into operation. Balance is not achieved by mere chance but is the end-result of intelligent study, which makes use of both our inner strengths and vulnerabilities.

We cannot completely free ourselves of our fears, desires, and anxieties except by death. But we can de-dramatize and tame them by better understanding their basic origin: birth, that sudden immersion in the imperfect.

8. *Action*

At one or the other extreme of its pendular movement the *self* is bound to ask: Does the world exist? For the all-important distinction between *self* and *non-self* is not defined once and for all. It is tested, verified, repeated, deepened, and explored all through life. The *non-self* is, indeed, even more mysterious than the *self,* which we know, or think we know, from the inside.

By its bulk and the problems it thrusts upon us the *non-self* can be so intrusive as to take us over. The *self* becomes cramped and withers away. Surely this is what happens to men who throw themselves too completely into their work.

Buddha's doubt of his Self and Descartes's doubt of the world come from the delicately balanced opposite poles of which we spoke in the last chapter. If I move toward independence and separation, my *self* comes on strong and the world fades out; if, on the contrary, I lean to fusion and belonging, then others capture and absorb me, and the *self* is diluted.

At each of these poles I soon feel a need and even a yearning for the other. During the most exciting journey I catch myself dreaming of idleness. After a few days of rest I long to get moving.

It's not because I'm unstable or have a tendency to be perpetually discontented. It simply demonstrates the fact that life is not equilibrium, but alternation.

The natural confrontation of the two poles, each reinforcing each other, is action.

The self cannot imagine the world per se. It becomes aware of it by either transforming it or being transformed by it.

This basically experimental attitude permits every man, educated or not, intelligent or not, to carry out the job of living. If we had to reflect before living we'd be paralyzed.

Does action, then, come before thought? Or is thought simply an interiorized form of action?

This question of action can be poignantly timely. We all know that our technological societies are built on *doing* rather than *being*. Nostalgically, we observe from afar those instances that remain of more passive and meditative civilizations. We feel certain that progress will soon dispel their silence, calm, and immobility just as it already has dispelled our own.

Without action we do not exist in relation to the world. But an overdose of action prevents us from existing within ourselves. Pascal challenged us to "stay quietly in one room." Unless we're nailed down by illness, we're not likely to do so. We moderns may wonder, then, if we are intoxicated by action to the point of losing the secret of repose.

At the least it would seem that we have no language other than action.

But is the need of action a modern aberration, a neurosis, or should it be admitted and experienced as being on a par with such necessities as breathing and eating?

Action bolsters the *self* by contributing to the permanence of its construction. Every act is a movement toward the *non-self* or else leans upon it. Thus, it contributes to the inevitable and indispensable effort to distinguish between the *self* and the world, tirelessly sharpening that boundary which has me on one side and the world on the other. Action perpetually singles me out.

The least of my projects uses some resources of the *non-self* (money, services, helpers). At the same time it defines me as the one who is carrying out the project and who completes it. Through the intermediary of the *non-self* I stand out as an individual.

While consolidating my autonomy every act also emphasizes separation and drives me further away from union with the rest of the Universe.

The powerful wind of action pushes me, then, toward the pole of separation. Those who wish to draw nearer to the opposite pole—union/fusion—strive to eliminate all action, to remain motionless, in a state of both outer and inner silence. Even so, action does not let itself be easily eliminated. Its inner wave, made up of thoughts and images, continues to batter the would-be meditative man and surreptitiously holds out its concreteness to him.

On the one side there is all the agitation of the world, to which my action responds; on the other, meditation. This highly symbolic battle is waged, obviously, on unequal terms. It is reasonable for the *self* to have some doubts as to its own existence. It cannot but feel unreal in the over-whelming presence of the *non-self,* which extends from what is nearest and most similar to myself, my children (and yet what differences there are between *us!*), to the farthest galaxy.

First of all, other people. The city crowds, the immea-surable numbers—five billion other earthlings. Then space—the immensity of the planet would crush us if we did not have artificial means (television, telephones, jet planes) to shrink it. As for the Cosmos, we can't even translate it into words, and its numbers are in the realm of sheer poetry. Who can conceive of the billions of stars in our galaxy alone?

Finally, time. A century seems long to us because it surpasses our life span, yet it is only a day in the history of mankind, a second in that of the Earth.

But the dimensions of our surroundings are not the only factors to surpass our understanding, making us insignifi-cant. The challenge of complexity, created by Man himself, is more direct and more daily.

This century has probably multiplied a hundred times the choices that every man has to make in his lifetime. The proliferation of knowledge, education, careers, products, amusements, personal contacts, and even signs, make us juggle a hundred balls.

And the stress of choice is no less intense than that of privation. Among the new constraints to which we are subject is one that cannot be escaped, that of making choices every day. The modern world casts aside and makes beggars of those who don't know how to use it. The village idiot has no longer any place to dwell. And the threat of rejection is added to that of complexity.

The more we list and analyze today's realities the more the task of measuring up to them seems overpowering. How shall we start? On what criteria are we to base our decisions? Even a limited view of all the options available to us at a given moment would be paralyzing.

A grain of sand cannot visualize the beach. Our puniness makes us unable to envisage reality except in fragments and symbols. If I think of my house I can't simultaneously call up its layout, the objects it contains, its general appearance, and the feelings I have for it. It would take me days to do so. So I limit myself to one or two aspects, those which fit in my momentary train of thought.

Although we fancy we can envisage reality, actually, like all other animals, we can only live it. Certainly the thinking process clarifies and focuses action, but it isn't thinking that has transformed the destiny of the human species; it is action, whether or not it has been thought out.

A cyclist defies the laws of gravity, but as long as he is pedaling he easily resists the forces of weight and inertia and moves along. Reality is simplified by action. Since action presupposes a single choice, it relegates the rest of reality to the background.

It is through action that we instinctively manage to scale the immense Universe down to our size.

Since the Universe cannot, by sheer intellect, be reduced to our dimensions, we act, in order not to be dizzied by it. If I want to go out in the evening I can't even begin to know all the possibilities that the city affords me. Merely listing them would take the whole night. And so, instinctively, I pick a category, films, for instance. Then my selective process starts with elimination. It is only when I have narrowed my choice to a single film that the evening's enjoyment begins.

So action is the *self's* only link to reality. And it plays an equally important role in our relationship to our *self*. Because every action, every choice or decision, strengthens the individuality of the man who effects it.

The pathological weakening of the *self*—the contemporary form of which is depression—is characterized by unwillingness and inability to act. In the gravest cases there is no urge to get up and wash and dress. I measure my good health by the energy of my actions. "I felt that I was really existing." Without action the *self* is purely potential.

The main source of the *self's* anxiety is not the overwhelming abundance of the surrounding world; it is, rather, nonexistence, *non-being*. We are speaking here not only of death, but also of nothingness, that black light of the unconscious, with our hesitating and stumbling silhouette outlined against it. We all fear death, but it is only the matter of a moment. It is what death conceals from us, the Beyond and its unfathomable nothingness, which leads us to suspect that life is only a brief respite from nonexistence, from this totally mysterious non-being.

The *non-self*, the outside world, threatens us with its infinity, but it exists and can be seen.

Non-being, however, is unapproachable: it is the chasm always beside us, which will inevitably swallow us up one day.

Its presence makes anxiety the natural human condition. Only action allows us to come to terms with it.

Because we cannot act upon the cause of anxiety, which

is our mortality, we combat its effects. But on fear we can act directly. If we are to undergo an operation, we can subdue our fear by telling ourselves that ninety-nine percent of those who had it come out alive. But when we are up against the absolute, which is the idea of non-being itself, we can only reduce our anxiety by averting our gaze. Action does change ideas and feelings and it appears to be the only therapy we have.

The plethora of the *non-self* and the emptiness of *non-being* have a common effect: they dissolve meaning. Every *self,* each protagonist in life, needs to seize the meaning, even the importance of what he says and does. For a long time our human meaning came from conformity to inherited values or from adherence to one or another recognized philosophy. Even when we have freed ourselves from these, we have not escaped from the essential psychological need.

So now it befalls us alone to rediscover for ourselves the ways of creating our own meaning.

The more we feel insignificant or fragile, the more meaning fades. A disappointment, a defeat, a rejection suffered at a moment when our *self* has a low visibility soon leads us to defeatist questioning, "What's the use?" But action restores meaning, or at least a semblance of meaning. And one or the other will do because, since our notion of meaning is subjective, we cannot tell the difference.

Of course we cannot be sure that the result of even a successful action will give us meaning. For that we should have to be certain of its value. This value may be established by a system, a code. The Moslem religion holds that it is good to prostrate oneself five times a day in the direction of Mecca. If we embrace this religion, this act will acquire a meaning for us, whereas, for a nonbeliever, it remains a mere gesticulation.

Value can be conferred from the outside, by someone whom we esteem and who has a value in himself. The lover offers his beloved some daisies. She exclaims, "What joy these give me!" So she has validated the act and given it meaning.

In both the above examples belief is necessary—religious or sentimental, whether love, friendship, affinity, comradeship. This belief derives from a previous decision of the *self* and validates the ensuing choices and acts which stem from them. When it comes to courage, the decision to believe is, we shall see, all-important.

Of course, a belief on the level of a bunch of daisies does not secrete a meaning adequate for a whole life. And at those moments when our very existence seems nearly absurd or insignificant it is difficult to find meaning in any of our actions.

That is, unless we endow the action itself with meaning. For the value of what it has achieved can always be called into question. Even our greatest feat, our masterpiece, can never attain perfection, because the shadow of non-being always overhangs it.

It's the fact of accomplishing an action, rather than its result, that brings us closest to a sense of unity.

To beat a record, to win an election, to publish a book, to obtain a contract, to bring pleasure to another's eyes, all these are tangible proof of our action upon reality. But, actually, we had found meaning a long time before, in all the preparations for these little triumphs.

Even if nothing comes of it, a well-conducted action

contains a value of its own. At least this is a reasonable and practical belief within the framework of a philosophy of the now.

Finally, it may well be that the necessity for action has a biological explanation in the disproportion between our brain and our body. Since our brain surpasses in riches and complexity the most advanced computer, it is plain that its flabby, disjointed container, the body, is primitive by comparison.

One of the great imbalances of our make-up is that our imagination far surpasses our physical ability to actualize it. This is why we have invented so many machines. We need extensions and protheses to embody our dreams. And even these are not enough.

Although the body easily wearies and seeks rest, the brain is still at it, all night, producing dreams. Because the brain commands the body, the latter reacts to reality and the evocation of reality in the same manner. The idea of danger provokes the same hormonal reaction as danger itself. Signs of sexual arousal are produced by mere thought, in the absence of objects of desire or even their visual representation.

The brain, all-powerful over its weak container, forces the latter into perpetual motion. Action ensues, almost mechanically. Faced with a problem our reflex is to try to solve it.

Isn't it often harder for us to do nothing than to do something?

It appears, then, that both physically and philosophically action is an intrinsic part of our nature and necessary to our well-being. It is useful and inevitable, it becomes neurotic only when we force it. Any useful machine can get out of control. The pressure for results favors such an aberration.

Action, which reflects the best in us, can reflect the worst as well. That is why contemporary Man badly needs a governor.

9. *Courage*

W<small>HEN</small>, <small>EXACTLY</small>, do I need courage? Contemplating or even deciding to carry out an action is not the same as doing it. A threshold, the level of which will vary, has first to be passed for my actions to take place. The proper unfolding of every day of my life depends on this crossing.

I advance toward the end of the diving-board, intending to jump. But suddenly the height seems too great and I hesitate. Shall I take the plunge? Inner debate, in which my self-concept, the memory of past dives, the way the wind is blowing and the gaze of the people around the swimming pool, all play a part. Whichever way I go, either plunging into emptiness or facing the sarcastic words of the onlookers and my own feelings of guilt, I need courage.

Courage impels me to move, *in spite of*. . . . When the goal is a pleasant one, there's no problem. I need no courage to raise a glass of water to my lips, that is, unless I've an arthritic arm, in which case it takes only a small amount of courage to raise it and drink, *in spite* of the pain.

Even when an action may be required or is of vital importance, it may run into resistances of all kinds. And if I am honest with myself, I shall see that the chief resistances are laziness and fear.

In laziness are all the hesitations that stem from the body: heaviness, passivity, torpor, the lack of tone or resilience. The body resists movement and change; it is reluctant to carry out immediately the orders transmitted by my will.

Fear gathers up the mind's resistances, which causes me, rightly or not, to be apprehensive about the results of the action on which I am about to embark.

Often laziness and fear work together, one bolstering the other to block our acting.

Is the moment of courage the passage to action in spite of laziness and fear?

This moment can be very short, but decisive. Once we have taken the plunge, the rest is a matter of the laws of gravity rather than courage. As soon as I have taken on someone by whom I've been intimidated, the rest of the conversation flows rather easily. The precise instant of courage can almost be isolated surgically, as if by a laser. It launches the action and then permits it to unfold without impediment.

Between desire and implementation there is a chain of inner attitudes that we know well.

I want a raise in my salary. I may play with the idea, talk to myself and even to others about it for some time.

From the wish, I move on to decision. I'll bring it up

with my boss on Tuesday while we're driving to meet a customer.

Here I am, sitting beside him while he tells me about last night's poker game. My request is on the tip of my tongue. But I have to interrupt him. Courage!

We can see at once the essential function of courage, which is to concretize. If I let the moment slip by, then my decision was not decisive, my will was only a whim and my desire remains floating in air.

Courage acts both on the future, which it causes to come about, and on the past, to which it gives, a posteriori, a direction.

Desire, will, decision, are all in the realm of intentions, and we have plenty of them. Only courage permits them to be enacted in reality.

Even when nothing of importance is at stake, the inception of movement brings courage into the picture. In order to clear the dinner table, duty takes the place of desire; will and decision join forces but nothing begins until I have the courage to get up and go to work.

We have situated courage and seen that point at which it intervenes. Now we must explore the question of what it is, then how to find and strengthen it. Just to have situated it at the beginning of action demonstrates how frequently it plays a part in our days. Indeed, it is a common component of life.

Literature and philosophy deal traditionally with great and noble examples: Socrates drinking hemlock, Turenne charging in spite of his trembling body, Guillaumet crossing the Andes in a blizzard "such as no beast would have faced."

Courage is usually thought to be the same as heroism

and virtue. It is offered to us as something exceptional and of great moral import.

This is why most people pay almost no attention to it. In our time, daily life is far removed from acts of heroism, and virtue is a subject for a sermon in church, which we no longer attend.

Commonplace courage, the kind we constantly need, is not particularly virtuous.

To live is neither good nor bad. And if all courage were heroic, every building on my street would be a Valhalla. Courage is, above all, a technique which I need in order to live. It may, of course, become an art, but very rarely does it border on the sublime. This technical aspect is important for the day-by-day practice of a courage made easy. But before we approach this most accessible and least disquieting aspect of courage, we must go a little further into its nature.

The key is the *in spite of,* which defines courage in terms of what it opposes. *In spite of* describes everything which goes to make up the contemporary, and eternal, difficulty of living.

What about the laziness we spoke about above? If the body prefers to lie down in a warm place rather than stand up in a cold one, if it prefers to be transported rather than to walk; if, in spite of its taste for sport, it is more inclined to passivity than to the expenditure of energy, there is a reason for it. Isn't its happiest memory that of the floating condition of its first nine months? Every expenditure of energy breaks it off from its former magic balance, every movement distances it from the perfect union with the world experienced in the motionless silence of the womb.

Our body's most direct and immediate enjoyment lies in the forgetfulness of self that comes from the feeling of being sustained, carried, taken care of. Here is oblivion to the world, the absence of variations of temperature, stimulation, and noise.

Of course, the prospect of stretching out under a coconut tree next July may cause the body, sparked by imagination and lashed by courage, to busy itself for months. We may give up immediate pleasures—such as sleeping late in the morning—for a deferred pleasure of greater magnitude—a vacation.

But this is a makeshift tactic. When we say, usually with a wistful sigh, "A man has to live," we are always comparing the moment of resignation to work and effort to a misty time when it was not so urgent to face up to reality. The daily necessity of living, eating, keeping our place in society and maintaining our relationships with others is a sharp descent into struggle as compared to the effortless happiness of earlier times.

In today's life the role of external reality is, perhaps, diminished.

My awareness of living is activated, through the senses, by impressions of external reality, but even more so by the permanent flow of mental images. These arise often from reality, but they constantly envelop it.

While I am holding a conversation, part of me is dedicated to getting the drift of what my interlocutor is saying and organizing my reply. But, at the same time, a stream of extraneous ideas and images flows through my mind.

The essential part of my life is dreamed or imagined, because the mind is quicker, more fertile, and more universal than the narrow range of sensory perceptions, more agile and imaginative than the body. It is also only in my thoughts that I am truly free. There no obstacles, dead weights, and resistances. The Universe is mine and, if such is my pleasure, I can be the whole Universe. It is only by imagination that I can draw close to contentment.

But even if reality plays a small role there is no getting around it. Over and over I must cope, either submitting to it or turning it to my own purposes. It is the diametrical opposite of imagination, and every contact with it implies choices, limits, and restrictions.

Yet, however difficult or painful, reality alone makes for health and well-being.

Before I set down these words, my mind thought up many others and dispersed itself in many confused directions, until finally I had to make a choice, to pin down my idea. Every writer is aware of the moment of putting pen to paper as a constraint (he's limiting himself to these poor words), but also as a liberation (after which he proceeds more freely).

Even in writing there is a thread of courage, the courage to have come down from the clouds of the imagination.

The gateway between dream and reality is that of courage.

Today when reality is rendered less restrictive by scientific and technical progress, when the imagery of the media envelops and impregnates us to the point of mingling with that of our own mind's creations, there is a great risk of loosening our moorings in reality. Many people, disappointed in the dull, mediocre nature of the day-to-day reality, let it become mere routine, almost outside their consciousness, and take refuge in imagination.

Courage to tear ourselves away from a dream-world is all the more necessary in that even the least confrontation with reality conceals within it the announcement of final defeat. Behind many demonstrations of laziness we can hear the words: "Hold off a moment, executioner!" To stall, to delay action, is to symbolically suspend the necessity of moving toward the future and hence toward death. If I don't move, perhaps I can stay the way I am and not grow old. Perhaps the Grim Reaper won't find me.

In a peaceful and comfortable society there is less frequent and imperious need of physical courage than of psychological courage (I prefer this last adjective to "moral," which sounds judgmental). The most current and also the most subtle *in spite of* is *in spite of my fears*. Often I feel an inner resistance to going ahead without immediately understanding or wanting to understand that the simple cause is fear.

Every human being is a formidable fear-factory.

There are reasonable fears, such as that which I feel sitting next to a drunkard driving at seventy-five miles an hour; generic fears such as agoraphobia and claustrophobia; constructive fears such as that which inspires us to put money aside.

To better understand what these fears have in common let us try to imagine that we are immortal. If we were sure that we would never die, what should we fear? Anything else can be overcome with time.

Every fear, conscious and identifiable, or unconscious, like that of a nightmare, has its roots in our anxiety about the destruction of our *self,* its annihilation by some visible or hidden power.

With most of us the fear of death is not constant. Few

of us think of it every day, and those who do aren't necessarily afraid. The fear of living, on the other hand, is to be found everywhere.

"Live it up!" is a popular phrase expressive of a down-to-earth philosophy. The more intensely we live—awake to everything, greedy for everything—the more we move, stir, create, and affirm ourselves, the more we achieve the autonomy that leads up to the final separation. If, on the contrary, our fear of life leads us to huddle up timorously in a corner, the days pass just as quickly but we are behaving as if, by living less intensely, we could stave off our death.

This explains the neuroses that banish some part of reality, the better to reduce our exposure to it and in doing so create our personal fortress against the assaults of anxiety. Everyone has a bit of a neurosis of this kind.

Behind my laziness and also behind my fear there is one and the same thing. My mortality.

This is what is covered by all of my *in spite of's,* what makes all my acts of courage indispensable and confers a touch of grandeur upon even the least of them.

To live, to affirm my existence even with the most elementary gestures, in spite of the presence, threat, certainty and irreducible mystery of death. This is not heroism, since it is a matter of our common fate; however, it takes courage. The more I am aware of where life is leading me, the greater need I have to take it on and to do that *in spite of everything.*

10. *Support*

C<small>OURAGE</small> <small>HELPS</small> <small>US</small> to move into action, to integrate ourselves with reality in spite of the awareness of our inescapable fate. It is an indispensable product, of fundamental necessity. Hence our need to find out on what it is based.

This search will lead us into metaphysics, but it begins with a problem of physics, pure and simple. If courage initiates a movement, by overcoming a resistance, then, it is a force which needs a support point. Now moral support does exist for us. Don't we, after all, *lean* on our principles?

For courage one can envision a whole range of support points, most of them very close to the movement to be undertaken. If a toothache keeps me awake, the courage to go have the tooth pulled is directly supported by the prospect of putting an end to my pain. Where the body is concerned things appear simpler.

In a number of everyday circumstances courage flows naturally and easily from one or another motivation. When we have a definite desire, the clear view of the end we wish to attain spontaneously puts the means of attaining it into operation. Thus, the effort to bridge the gap between ourselves and the object of our desire or aspiration has only a very slight element of courage about it.

The ideal courage "made easy" is the one of which we are not even aware. If my daughter is drowning before my eyes, I shall risk my life to save her, but the motivation is so overwhelmingly strong that my entrance into the reality of the rough seas proceeds with almost as much ease as it would in my imagination. The question may legitimately arise: Was there any courage involved *at all*?

If, along with my daughter, one of her friends is in danger as well, wouldn't real courage begin when I go to rescue *her*?

Here again, we find the old courage-virtue: To speak of courage, it has to be hard-won, it has to hurt.

So let us consider the degrees, and not only of its existence. A father who hardly knows how to swim shows more courage by throwing himself into the water than does a professional lifeguard. (If he can't swim at all then he's foolhardy rather than courageous.) In both cases there is a passage into action, confrontation with a reality which may entail the sacrifice of a life. There is, then, courage, even if there are also circumstances that favor it.

Whether courage is implicit or self-conscious, whether it is supported by obvious or more direct motivations, the fundamental question is that of the ultimate courage. We can't be sure of facing up to life's unpredictable and difficult events if we have not come to grips with the problem of our own death.

Easier said than done! Who can be sure of this achievement? Even the great mystics—as Luther recognized—have found themselves unexpectedly seized by overpowering *angst*. The *self* is mobile; it wavers and fluctuates even when there is no wind, and all the more so when circumstances put it to the test.

The prospect of death is such an integral part of life that, after a certain age (usually between thirty-five and forty-five years), we are all confronted with the question of our final destination.

Immortality, return to nothingness, reincarnation, fusion with the Universe—for the twenty or thirty thousand years that men have lived with the unknowable they have not greatly broadened the range of hypotheses.

From childhood on, our personal temperament (the nature and intensity of our fears), our upbringing, education, and cultural background, lead us to choose among the above alternatives. If we never re-examine our choice it may not withstand a rude existential blow (the death of a loved one, a threat to our own life, a period of depression). If we have not deliberately meditated on our own death we may be forced, rather roughly, to do so by the unexpected occurrence of one of these natural but tragic events.

For my part, it is not out of morbid delight that I emphasize the necessity of thinking through our own death. It is seldom mentioned, even among close friends. Only a few people except church-goers heed or echo the warning about our mortality sounded by religious groups over the centuries.

The failure to face up to it is fraught with too-obvious dangers. An urban and mercantile society holds up to us only the search for happiness/well-being (the distinction is purposely blurred), founded on what the ancient Greek philosophers already called the pleasure principle.

To maximize pleasure and minimize pain calls for no special schooling or ideology; it is a profound animal instinct. But every pleasure erodes, even if only a little; enough, in any case, to show it can't be the reason for our existence. The frantic, often pathetic effort to rediscover the intensity of youth and its fresh feeling usually leads to some form of disgust and meaninglessness.

Depression notoriously blocks our capacity to find enjoyment or meaning in anything at all. It is only as unbearable as it is contemporary. And the risk of losing the meaning of life is very real if we refuse to question ourselves about our end, to forge a personal philosophy.

The ultimate courage is the willingness to sacrifice our own existence. It is that rock on which all other possible kinds of courage can be based.

If it is not potentially there, all other courages may collapse when we need them most. But there is no proof that this first and indispensable step is painful. If I manage to take it, all the rest will be facilitated. If not, I shall be left at the mercy of my anxieties. To be reconciled with my death means to admit its reality and make peace with it. After a peace treaty we usually live better.

In a recent film a Japanese soldier, on the point of being executed, explains, "Before leaving for the war I decided I was already dead. That way I lived through combat without trembling. There is no reason why I should tremble any more today." This attitude is part of the martial arts of Japan; it comes from the *bushido,* or moral code, of the *samurai.*

It has been rediscovered and elaborated today by psychologists who study the art of decision making. They note that, before undertaking something important, the ablest decision-makers first clearheadedly envisage the failure of their project. Not out of pessimism but, rather, to make sure that, if failure there is, they will have readied the resources of defenses to cope with it.

Once the possibility of failure is recognized, they can concentrate all the more confidently on the chances of success and advance boldly toward the accomplishment of their aim. To look catastrophe in the face is to grapple courageously with our fear.

No one values life cheaply. Quite spontaneously we put its preservation among our top priorities. And yet, no. It is not really the first among them.

Should we respect anyone who would choose to sacrifice his honor or the life of his dear ones rather than accept his own death? Not too easily. A sign that we would rather not see ourselves as cowards.

In our personal scale of values, then, the preservation of life at any cost does not hold the highest rank. Even without an explicit decision we are probably ready, under a certain limited number of real circumstances, to make the sacrifice. Hoping that we shall never have to, of course, not sure that we won't.

Here is the ultimate courage, present, from time immemorial, in every man. We have only to recall the plays, operas, legends, and other literary works of all times and places. The phrase "*I'd rather die than . . .*" echoes from one work to another and in the depths of our own being. It is like the button to be pressed for collective atomic suicide in the cellars of the Elysée Palace or the White House. It is understandable, of course, that most of us would rather not linger in those cellars.

Within us, however, is the "hard core," the essential support point for the more ordinary forms of courage. And to take death into account, to look at it without fear, gives us access to an essential force.

We die only once, but we live every day. Every life bears in it a varied amount of evil, suffering, and tragedy. If I strengthen my position in regard to death I consolidate my ability to face the negative and meaningless elements of life, which I run into more frequently than I do the Grim Reaper.

Most people draw up a will and take out life and health insurance. But these measures are of a legal and financial nature and are not matched on the moral and psychological level.

This is because these two apparently parallel lines of action are, in reality, diametrically opposite to one another. When I take out an insurance policy I hope to free myself from a number of life's hazards, as if I were exorcizing misfortunes by paying for the prevention of their occurrence. The Church saw the possibilities of this type of bargaining when it sold indulgences, guarantees against consignment to Purgatory. Products for an insurance salesman!

To admit life's tragic dimension, from mere rheumatism to death, means, on the contrary, to take it upon ourselves, to realize that it is not transferable to others but inherent in our solitude. It means deciding to live, in spite of everything and, indeed, all the more fully.

The message we get from the contemporary world, where the canons of advertising have been substituted for those of the Church, is that, in order to be happy, we must have everything that Faust asked of Mephistopheles—eternal youth, power, riches, charm, and intelligence. Every young would-be executive, climbing the ladder of his promising career, makes touching effort to win all these prizes.

Alas, even if we grant that such efforts may yield some short-term happiness, the prospects are very slim for the long run. And there is the further danger that if even a single element among them is lost, the whole meaning of life may collapse or drop away.

I believe that I am better equipped by recognizing from the beginning the presence in my life of frailty, anxiety, solitude, ignorance, and inadequacy.

My wager, that I can find some happiness *in spite of* these unlikeable companions, cannot be won in advance, but it seems more promising, in the long view, than an attempt to pin down the barometer at "Steady Good Weather."

To base our courage on the clear-sighted acceptance of the negative side of life means to take out insurance against a sudden loss of meaning. What remains is to build up, to act in the realm of the positive.

11. *Force*

The courage of ultimate sacrifice, that is our life jacket. After we've been shown how it works, it's reassuring to know that it's under the seat. But we count on not having to use it.

In daily life, as well as under extraordinary circumstances, we must bring force to bear in order to initiate an action. The more dramatic the force, the easier the passage to action will be. We often hear tired people say, "I've lost heart," by which they mean energy. If we are to draw on our energy, the body must be in good health. Otherwise, the courage required for even the simplest act is out of all proportion.

Courage comes from the Latin word *cor,* heart, and this derivation is enough to show that it belongs to the realm of affect, emotion, not of logic. When we must start moving, reason is of limited aid. It may emphasize, confirm, and justify the difficult first step, but it is powerless to trigger it.

Leaders of every stripe—politicians, generals, and business-men—know from experience that any decision is more a matter of feeling than of logic.

For no decision can be based on complete information. Even after the most costly preliminary studies and reworked scenarios, we know only a part of the context and can only guess at outcomes. Nonetheless, we must decide, we must place our bets on the squares of reality with our eyes as wide open as possible.

Nor can courage be fitted into an equation. I can't *prove* to a friend that he must show courage, but I can try to strengthen his motivation, to recharge him with positive prospects.

What is the nature of the force that gives us courage? Have we, perhaps, hit the mark in speaking of *the desire to live*? As it is a widespread resource in the animal world, it would seem that man would be able to draw easily on it. Unfortunately, the complex relationship between our mind and emotions often causes regrettable losses of this desire. Since the days of the oil embargoes, great progress has been made in the management of energy. On the basis of the same simple principles, can't we try to lay out an economic strategy for dealing with the various forms of courage?

First, the carrier of the energy must be in the best possible condition. Second, no possible source of energy—even the most modest—must be neglected. Finally, this precious resource must be used with maximum intelligence.

I am the carrier. How, then, do I judge my condition?

The answer must come from three indissoluble but distinct aspects of human nature.

For two thousand years we have spoken of the dichotomy between body and spirit. Today, it seems more appropriate to substitute a threefold image: body, mind, and affect.

Until the present century this last was viewed with ignorance or scorn, although we well know that it is the key factor of our equilibrium. In other days, moreover, little attention was paid to the body; it had simply to be fed. Exercise amounted to no more than the exertion required by work and by the journey from one place to another. When the body began to deteriorate there was little to be done; people resigned themselves to a declining condition of life.

The mind, on the other hand, from the earliest times, has been the object of attention and training. From ancient Egypt up to the nineteenth century, only the privileged class benefited from a systematic education. But it was already recognized that no man could realize his full potential without the systematic exploitation of his mental faculties.

Nowadays, in all modern countries, education has become the foremost national undertaking. But there is still a tendency to interpret the word "education" as applying only to the development of the mind.

Only for a single generation has there been a serious interest in the maintenance of the body. First we had to take notice of the physical ravages characteristic of the present day: excessive food, unused and atrophied muscles, and nervous stress. These things are not fatal; but many people, while still young, have suffered their handicaps.

Today there is widespread awareness of health. People are eating, drinking, and smoking less; more than half the population of the United States goes in for regular physical exercise. The increased purchase of health care items weighs heavily on the family budget. Our generation is obsessed with their bodies. But this is a phase necessary to make up for the previous neglect of both health and appearance, which eroded, in turn, the desire to live.

So the mind has long been an object of our care, and now the body has become one. But the third factor, so necessary to our equilibrium, has not yet received its due.

The affect remains a sort of black box, which is little known, badly managed, and therefore gives us constant trouble.

Its content of passions, desires, emotions, sensibilities, and humors is quite different from that of the mind, with its knowledge, reflection, reasoning, and deduction. But, because the components interact with one another (a mood can block or intensify reflection; an idea can arouse an emotion), they are constantly confused.

Few of us can distinguish, within ourselves, between what is ruled by the mind and what is ruled by feeling. We were not taught to do so in the course of our formal education, and have to learn by trial and error and by experience, and often by pain.

Studies in pathology broke ground in this area. Freud brought about recognition of affect's primordial importance and drew a map of it. The ideas, vocabulary, and culture of the affective realm are still in the hands of therapists who strive to correct its disorders.

The situation is the same as that which prevailed, until recently, for the body. We pay little attention to our affect unless it gives us trouble and we feel the need of consultation. Once medical doctors were comical figures; their hermetic formulas made us laugh in much the same way as many do at the vocabulary and practices of the shrinks.

Most often we simply note that some people are emotionally stable while others are subject to broad swings (not to mention those who are obviously disturbed). Just so, once upon a time people were either thin or fat and little could be done about it. It is, surely, not absurd to imagine that if we can exercise and transform the body and mind, we can have a similar influence on our affect.

We have learned to have clear ideas and to cultivate good health. In order to achieve this we pay attention to subtle details of our life-style and treat our bodies like the precision instrument that it is. But we have the helpless apprehension that the expected benefits of this considerable effort can suddenly be swept away by some frustration or eroded by an ill-defined anxiety.

To achieve a technology of the *self* we must be able to act on our three aspects simultaneously. Affective good shape exists; it can be searched for, rediscovered, and kept up by a number of means.

Where our courage is concerned, the search for good affective form has two beneficial consequences. The greater my dynamism the easier it is to mobilize my emotional resources in order to effect the passage to action. When we are in good affective form we are less subject to fears, more inclined to optimism, attitudes which are thought to "spark courage."

More important still, if I maintain my affective shape it means that I've better understood my own mechanisms and strengthened my self-control. Everything that gives me a feeling of greater mastery over my own life increases confidence in my ability to deal with unexpected or delicate situations. Who could fail to be encouraged?

How then are we, in practice, to keep our affect in good health? We lack a model.

Intellectual performance is evident in its results. Thinkers, strategists, and scientists offer us a broad and varied choice of champions.

As for models of physical achievement, we have all too many. Beautiful faces and bodies are tirelessly presented to us by those willfully optimistic mirrors of ourselves, magazines and television.

Models of harmonious affect, however, are scarcer. They cluster around two themes: abnegation and, as it happens, courage. The first are religious or religiously minded: saints, gurus, great humanitarians. St. Francis of Assisi, Gandhi, and Albert Schweitzer all gave up the pleasures of ordinary life in order to serve a nobler cause. But if the truth be told, the most frequent reaction to the names of these sublime figures is a feeling of guilt rather than a desire to imitate them.

Models of courage are more varied and more apposite. Athletics furnishes many examples, not only of physical courage (of which soldiers have even more) but also of stubborn persistence in the training of the body.

People are coming to be less interested in pure exploits and more in the discipline and training that precedes them. Here we have a shift of emphasis that has many implications for the future.

The ethical courage most boosted by the media is that of moral witnesses, people more willing to give up their own freedom than renounce their principles of them. Andrei Sakharov is today the epitome.

But saints, champions, and heroes are models of virtue rather than of balanced living. They represent extreme situations, far from our own searches and humbler ambitions. I am happy and proud that they have striven to ennoble the human race, since I am a member of it. But, unless one of them happens to be part of our own crowd, we are not likely to them. Let us try, rather, to sketch the portrait of an average autonomous individual, standing solidly on his own two feet, and generally content with his life.

In order to find in ourselves the courage needed at any given moment, we must combine, in varied doses, five inner forces: self-direction, disidentification, the ability to deal with anxiety, desire, and gratification.

SELF-DIRECTION

I choose my aims, my criteria for success, my refusals, on the basis of my own personal system of values rather than on those that others, or the world around me, propose.

If we go by set moral or religious codes, advertising messages, family pressures, or the urge to "keep up with the Joneses," then we are other-directed. This is the habitual situation of a young child, of anyone living under an authoritarian government, and of one of the faithful (not to be confused with a believer). But it is also that of a spellbound consumer, a sheep-like party voter, a timorous worker, and an opportunistic, demagogical, or accommodating executive. All of these are to a certain extent prey to the fear of making a mistake, disappointing, or not coming up to expectations. Their attitude bodes no good for affective health.

Of course, my inner-directed system of values is largely composed of elements drawn from the outside (none of us is called upon to reinvent the world). But a process of personal growth allows me to absorb them in a way consonant with my own inclinations and experiences.

Such inner direction is not common. A study made by the Stanford Research Institute concludes that the inner-directed are no more than twenty percent of the country's population.

DISIDENTIFICATION

If someone scrapes one of my car's fenders and I get out with the intention of cursing or even striking him, it is because I identify myself with my car. Many objects in our still primitive society lend themselves to such feelings. A threat to them is a threat to me.

A boy is arrested for shoplifting at the dime store and his mother is called down to the police station. When she sees her son she asks: "How could you do this to *me*?" Obviously she identifies with him.

Disidentification is the basic gymnastics of the *self*. It demands that, within us, we constantly step backward or to one side in order to distinguish that which is genuinely part of our *self* from that which is episodic and contingent.

My family, *my* problems, *my* possessions; too often I confuse them with myself. As soon as there is some difficulty in their regard I get emotionally involved because I mistakenly identify with them. No good for the affective form.

There is no question, naturally, of going so far as to say that our neighbor's distress should leave us indifferent simply because it is not ours. To love means to partially identify, of our own free will, with another. But even then it is healthier for both him and me to pause and think out how best to help him rather than to brood and thus add my suffering to his.

COMING TO TERMS WITH ANXIETY

This is harder; there is no all-embracing solution, and only a minimum of advice that can be given. Anxiety is inherent in the human condition. It is existential in character.

Usually we manage to avert our eyes and try not to think about it. But it makes unexpected reappearances, sometimes at the worst possible moments. We have already proposed trying to approach anxiety clearheadedly, at least to take the measure of its intensity to know our personal means of facing up to it. Such means do exist (since we all live and many manage to keep smiling).

To better direct this meditation, let us only note that it is wise to keep in mind the three great sources of anxiety which we cannot avoid. They correspond to the three "existential questions" mentioned in Chapter 3.

DEATH

Already discussed, and the most obvious. Linked less to death itself, which may turn out to be peaceful, than to uncertainty about what is beyond. This is the anxiety from which all others derive.

REJECTION

With or without religion, the sense of good and evil is an integral part of our mental structure, of which we are aware from our earliest childhood. It is linked with the panicky fear of rejection, whose origin is to be sought in the first separation, that of birth. As we face our fellow beings, quite alone, we are prey to the nightmare of their condemnation, which contains the risk of exclusion, of being cut off from the sources of human warmth on which we depend.

MEANINGLESSNESS

The most contemporary anxiety, sparked by the disappearance of religious and ideological supports. The search for a meaning to life has fallen upon our shoulders. What makes this anxiety difficult to manage is the fact that the need for meaning is reborn in us every day. We may find a number of answers, at different levels, but meaninglessness has become the most widespread and pernicious form of anxiety.

Every one of these existential questions can directly attack our affective or emotional component. There is no way to stand off their assaults. Failing any guarantee or miracle cure, the only mature attitude is to absorb them, to take them on, in the knowledge that we must live with them, and to make ready appropriate responses.

DESIRE AND GRATIFICATION

If envy is on the list of the deadly sins, it shows that the Church cared more about restraint than about marketing. Certainly, unbridled desire and envy can imprison us and cause us to suffer. The wise man's ideal is the absence of desire, which is accompanied by complete detachment. But Occidentals do not seem to have evolved to the point of approaching, in great numbers at least, this final stage.

A desire to live is the best sign of affective health; the display of desires, large and small, gives color to our emotional well-being.

"There's nothing I want" is, indeed, the first symptom of depression.

Desire should not only be stripped of every trace of guilt-feeling, it should be cultivated like a vegetable garden. To scatter our days with occasions of desire, often modest or purely personal in nature, is to pass through them more lightly, just as we cross a river by leaping from one stone to another. A satisfied desire, a gratification which we make a gift of to ourselves—there is no better way of reviving our joy of living.

Because even when courage has to face up to worst threats and anxieties, it cannot renew its strength in either asceticism or suffering. Like every form of human energy, courage wears out unless we grant it respites and satisfactions. Nothing is better for the muscle tone of the affect than success. Good marks, compliments, and applause are the healing balm of the soul.

If courage permits action, then success in action is a better tribute to courage than erecting a monument to it.

The man or woman with an ideally balanced affect can branch out in many directions. He has a clear view of his goals, knows how to enjoy himself, and takes care to savor his successes. If he loves someone, he knows, instinctively, what is good and what is bad for the object of his love; and, on this basis, he accents the former and diminishes the latter. The cultivation of his affective component, which, in its turn, generates courage, comes down to observing himself as he would a stranger and treating himself frankly as he would treat someone he loves.

12. *Ease*

THERE ARE PLENTY of reasons why we should make the best possible use of our energy-courage. We have only to look at our nature, which adjusts very easily to the law of least effort. This is true especially when giving in to laziness or procrastination leads us into situations that take not courage, but heroism, to get out of.

We have seen ordinary laziness as a deterrent to action. But the courageous man may practice a good kind of laziness by seeking simplification. To use our head to save the effort of our legs, and our mind to spare our emotions, lightens life and adds grace to it. To filter and refine is an aesthetic process. In art, as in life, to lay it on thickly usually betrays a lack of inspiration.

More fundamentally, low-voltage courage affords us the best chance of personal progress and development. Whatever demands a strong dose of courage from me usually indicates the limits of my capacity. If my timidity makes it as hard for me to enter a crowded room as it is for another man to jump out of the trenches, it's a sign that my address-book is very slender.

Contrary to current preaching, what is difficult is not necessarily praiseworthy.

Sometimes, yes, because life has its dramas. But in everything pertaining to my customary activities—work, relations with others, the care of my body—the necessity of calling upon courage may be a bad sign. If there were such a thing as a courage meter, a rising needle would indicate a block or a neurotic zone.

The search for "easy" or casual courage is not primarily intended to make life more agreeable and rid us of guilt. It is, rather, a philosophical attitude. To extend the limit of everyday courage enables me to extend myself, to gain a broader vision of what I can do with my life.

In many cases this happens quite naturally. In my profession, in sports, or when I have to communicate, acts which, the first time, demanded courage become familiar with repetition. The acts are the same. But, with habit, the mountain I made of them is leveled. Hence the passage to action is no longer a problem.

There are, however, areas where we make little progress even with the passage of time. And, above all, there are always new problems to be dealt with.

Take the common case of fear. Sometimes we don't even realize that whatever delays the accomplishment of an action such as a difficult telephone call is not the lack of time but the fear of not knowing what to say or of meeting with a refusal.

There are three possible attitudes to take before that of fear: letting ourselves be overpowered and failing to act; acting with courage, in spite of everything; and losing our fear.

The classical texts of the Stoics concerning courage say that the man who does not act is a coward and the man who has no fear has no merit. Thus, in order to prove our courage, we should tremble and advance at the same time.

In the majority of life's situations, common sense is a virtue more useful than courage. And common sense suggests that the best attitude is to be unafraid.

The better we know how to use courage, the more we choose to use it in only homeopathic doses. Ever since David and Goliath, skill has been set against force. Why not aim at having and using both?

If life is incarnated through action (which includes the simple act of thinking), and if every passage to action involves courage, then to live well and freely means passing to action as easily as possible, without fanfare.

To de-dramatize courage, to reduce it to something commonplace so that we are no longer aware of its mechanisms, this should be our reasonable and attainable aim. In order to achieve it we need a bit of courage, to be sure. But that we expected.

The problem is this: To overcome any resistance to action more easily. In physical terms, we can envisage different approaches—to break up the resistance, to level it, to get ourselves pulled from the other side of the obstacle in order to go effortlessly through it, or else to go around it by some other path. In psychological terms we may add an even wider range of solutions, from realizing the resistance to perceiving that it does not exist.

The techniques of casual or "easy" courage are no more mysterious than such as these. They stem more often from peasant wisdom than from highbrow philosophy. If now we must study them it is because we are no longer peasants and not yet philosophers.

Everything takes place in the realm of the affect, since courage is one of its components whose purpose is to overcome the others: fear, suffering, laziness, and so on.

It is supremely important to learn to distinguish a given problem from the emotion which it triggers in us.

On the eve of an examination I may feel that I am more or less well prepared. On another level, I may be a little, very, or not at all anxious. To deal with the problem I must foresee it, I must first put into action the courage to cram. But however well prepared I may be, I must deal also with my emotions; that is, I must try to sleep well and to stay cool after I've finished cramming.

In both procedures, and they may present themselves together, I will have reduced the dose of courage necessary for the examination morning.

Two possible approaches exist, two levels of action for applying "easy" courage to both the problem and my emotion. At one level I can reduce the problem to routine, cut it down and transform it. At the other level I can refocus and transform the emotion.

ROUTINE

Routine suffers from bad press; it calls up everything tiresome and boring. We choose to endure it as briefly as possible. But we can't function by rediscovering reality every quarter of an hour. Part of our activities are routine in order to save us from having to make constant decisions. We don't "decide" every morning to brush our teeth; it's a matter of habit. Most everyday problems are met with reactions that have turned into reflexes.

Everyone knows that a sedentary body should be exercised in order to remain healthy and attractive. But few of us do anything about it. Sports are very fine, but the courts are far away, the games are expensive and complicated, and very often it's raining. But twenty minutes of exercise in one's own room do more good than a couple of hours of tennis or bicycling per week. No rain falls and it takes only the courage to make up one's mind to do it for a month or two, after which time it becomes as routine as brushing your teeth.

When people hear that you do such a workout every day they see you as being very courageous. But you know that it took just a small amount of courage a long time ago.

Some people need courage to read, and reproach themselves for not reading enough. A routine half-hour of reading a day leads to the consumption of a whole shelf at the end of a year. If you learn to select your books, habit will soon change courage into pleasure.

CUTTING DOWN

Routine creates an area of time which is to be regularly occupied in a certain way until further orders. The practice of cutting down carries out a similar prescription but is applied to a single task which otherwise would be too much for me.

I haven't the courage to sit down and write a book, but perhaps I have enough to write four pages a day which, in fifty days, comes to two hundred pages. I haven't the courage to learn to play the guitar, but I have enough to take two lessons a week. I'll never find the twenty or thirty hours necessary for making a marketing study, but I can work on it two mornings a week for a month.

All of us have a concentration span, beyond which our attention and perseverance drop off precipitously. To concentrate for any length of time beyond our personal capacity seems to call on us for considerable courage. With a bit of cunning we can almost always cut a task into pieces small enough for us to handle without pain. This, says an Indian proverb, is how a man manages to eat an elephant.

In the above examples small acts of courage were more accessible, more easily performed than a great one. But there are cases where the contrary is true.

TRANSFORMATION

Here too it is a matter of dealing with the problem of acting upon reality. Too often I tend to think that reality is presenting me with too many situations with which I must deal. As the number of demands upon me—from my profession to my family, friends and even my budget—pile up, my automatic response is to cope, up to the limit of my capacity for absorption. When suddenly the smallest acts call for a maximum of courage, then I know that I am overloaded.

It is much easier to cut down the demands from the outside by a third than it is to increase my ability to deal with them in the same proportion. Almost always, a close scrutiny of my supposed obligations enables me to take a second look and perform a salutary weeding-out.

I can delegate more office responsibilities to my subordinates, rediscuss family constraints, and relieve myself of peripheral activities. Often behind the phrase "I have to" there lurks the question, "How can I get out of it?"

To go on trying to keep up with everything is a waste of courage and hence of *self*. Here, a major act of courage, such as transforming the whole situation, may save us from performing the myriad smaller acts necessary to keep things going as before.

This is notably the case in what we might call the blind alleys of existence, the tight spots where we find ourselves with our backs against the wall in an increasingly painful situation. Here it seems to take more and more courage just to survive from day to day.

Divorces, separations, firings, resignations, surgical operations, selling one's house, all these commonplace turning-points call for a mountain of courage. Rightly so, because the decision to effect any one of them strikes near the roots of our emotions. Often they involve severing a part of ourselves, whether physical or affective.

But usually, after we have taken the plunge, the relief and obvious benefits are such that we only wish we had done so earlier.

To get out of our emotional blind alleys is equivalent, in private life, to heroism in battle.

These moments, which obviously demand a surge of courage, show a man that he can face up to his destiny. Not only has he staunched the bleeding of minor courages, but he has also advanced by another notch in the achievement of his autonomy.

REFOCUSING

The most spectacular way in which we conserve courage is not to modify the problem but to transform the emotion that it provokes in us.

Our ignorance, fears, and neuroses refract the obstacles in our path the way the water of an aquarium deforms the shapes of the fish swimming in it. They cause us to see them as much larger than they really are. Refocusing aims at restoring, as far as possible, their true proportions.

Don't we often consider only the difficulties, risks, and painful aspects of a given action? To take a new look at it, from a positive viewpoint (there always is something positive, if only the good riddance to a tedious task), eases the passage to action.

The positive use of the imagination has recourse to a real technique, that of *visualization,* which great athletes employ at the moment of their boldest feats. Instead of thinking: "the bar is too high" or "the pressure's too much" (which is probably true), they try to see themselves as concretely as possible accomplishing their exploit. In their minds they project the film of their mounting the platform to receive the prize; they caress the medal when it is awarded to them. When they reach the obstacle they actually jump higher.

Through visualization we link the action to be undertaken to the future, the site of our hopes and expectations which are almost here. An energy is released which pushes us forward and over the slope to be climbed, the obstacle to be jumped over.

Just as a positive anticipation can be simulated by refocusing the future, so a negative one can be attenuated by a similar operation directed toward the past.

All of us, in the process of living, have won out over many difficulties, resolved many problems, crossed stormy seas without sinking. The composure of old soldiers is based on memories like these.

Just as we are about to plunge into a new adventure we must not let stress make us forget to turn the projector onto a past which we have come through with fair success. We need to gain perspective on our coming task or trial by comparing it to previous episodes that turned out much better than we had feared would be the case.

To this refocusing on what lies ahead and what went before we may add a glance to the side. Most of the readers of this book, as well as its author, lead in this latter period of the century relatively privileged lives.

We do not live in totalitarian countries, we know neither hunger nor poverty, few of us are incurably ill. We simply live in ignorance or forgetfulness of our good fortune.

Of course we may say to our children, "It's shameful to leave half your meat on the plate when, this very evening, millions of little Africans have nothing to eat." This is an easy way to make them feel guilty, but quite useless, since probably they are not old enough to have a planetary conscience. But *we* have it.

It's a matter of philosophical decency not to exaggerate our own torments and problems. A difficult demand, but one which, by enlarging our stature, lends us strength.

This lateral refocusing is relevant not only to those less well provided for than ourselves but also to our peers. When we are anxious at the prospect of a difficult or new passage just ahead, then a quick thought to the many other people, elsewhere, who are in the same situation and are going to come through, may lead us to the healthy question: "Why not me?"

To refocus means to dance, like a boxer, around our problem until we find the proper angle, the passage, the breach which will enable us to win with the least expenditure of courage.

COMPENSATION

Another way of playing on the emotion that generates courage is to consciously increase the muscle tone of the *self* of which we spoke at the end of the preceding chapter. The more positive our psychological context is, the more easily courage will come to us.

In order to brighten our inner life, aside from such spectacular but short-lived events as love-at-first-sight, a winning lottery ticket, or election to public office, we may profitably recall some of grandmother's recipes.

REWARDS

Rewards cultivate personal pleasure. Many people think they're strong because they are harsh with themselves. But it has not been established that they live any the better.

SUCCESS

Its galvanizing role can't be exaggerated. Hunger for approval is as widespread as sexual desire. Although genuine success can't be invented or won on easy terms, we can pursue it by picking up only such challenges as we are capable of meeting. The worst enemy of success is overweening ambition. If we aim at impossible goals we are sure to make what might have been a remarkable performance into a psychological defeat.

ECLECTICISM

Nature ensures the perpetuation of the species by generosity and redundancy. Specialization and lack of time cause modern man to live too harshly. If one of his essential aspects breaks down, the whole *self* threatens to crumble. Of course, to keep up a multiplicity of interests, pleasures, contacts, and activities—in short, satisfactions—requires a planned effort. But the security of our affect is worth the price.

SUPPORT NETWORKS

The people who emerge best from the vicissitudes of life are those who have a supportive human environment. Such a network—made up of family, friends, colleagues, loved ones, and casual companions—doesn't come into being or hold fast without an effort on our part. If we are to combat the contemporary tendency to withdrawal and isolation, we must be aware of the hard work required of us. Autonomy, as in the true sense, is almost always impractical in complete solitude. Not everyone can be a hermit. A support network relieves us of searching afar for models, motivations, affection, help, advice, connections with other resources, challenges, and . . . spectators.

The conclusions of a psycho-medical study of individuals who have best survived life's stresses prove that we have been on the right track in the preceding pages.

1. These individuals don't tend to become obsessed by a problem; they "set it aside" until they feel that they can deal with it.

2. They shift their attention (or modify the rhythm of their day) after any tense or nerve-wracking moment. They turn to sport or some other activity, or simply relax.

3. They maintain a panoramic view of their whole life and do not let themselves be submerged by the details of a single situation.

4. Because they know how to plan, they foresee difficulties and don't allow themselves to be taken by surprise.

5. They face up to problems directly, even the most disagreeable among them.

6. They know their own limitations and pick no challenges they can't meet.

7. When they come up against a difficulty they look for causes rather than scapegoats.

8. They are capable of accepting a certain unpopularity and don't torment themselves over what other people may think about them.

9. They don't set for themselves impossible deadlines but know how to calculate the time necessary to complete a given action.

10. They purposely limit the role that work plays in their life, because they are concerned, above all, with their balance.

The study does not say whether these individuals come by courage more easily than others, but realistic and well-balanced as they are, this seems self-evident. So here we are, close to a concrete blueprint of the technology of self-management.

13. *Everyday Courage*

I<small>S THERE A SINGLE COURAGE</small> or are there different kinds? Shall we compare it to energy, in which case it matters little whether it is thermal, nuclear, or hydraulic, whether it serves for heating or to power a motor? We can't hold a practical discussion of energy problems without recourse to a theory of equivalences quite independent of its applications. But this lies in the field of physics, not of psychology.

Since courage is an affect, perhaps we should ally it to the most celebrated of affects, love, which does not lend itself to conceptualization. No matter how powerfully we are exhorted to go for universal love, we have a hard enough time analyzing the proportions of mother-love, brotherly love, love of neighbor, and falling-in-love love. Just as these varieties of love are experienced very differently, perhaps we should also see kinds of courage as so diverse that they have nothing but the word that covers them in common. So far, in our efforts to free courage from the moralizing mist in which it has always been enveloped, we have chosen to generalize.

This is because every passage to act *in spite of* must be triggered by a release of this affect. As soon we are aware of it, we spontaneously call it courage.

But if psychological and philosophical reasoning helps us to put order into our thoughts, it also removes us from the concrete. It calls up abstractions and mental processes which have the same relation to our experience as does a map of Chicago to walking in the city's streets. The map is a help, it keeps us from getting lost, but it obviously doesn't replace our footwork.

For everything that touches upon my daily life, direct and specific experience counts much more than reasoning. To understand courage as a form of energy helps me along the way. But when I consider courage in its applications it seems to me, by its diversity, to be more like love.

The trouble with the specific is that if we start to depict all its facets we see no end to it. Our life situations are infinite in numbers. We must be satisfied with a rough-and-ready idea, the first plunge into the concrete, which every one of us can pursue on his own account, in his own measure.

There is a courage for all the ages but the varieties of it most pertinent to us are those necessary to contemporary man, such as we saw him in the beginning of this book.

Thus we shall speak only for memory's sake of the kind

of courage which had individually been held of prime importance (especially for the male of the species), the courage to fight.

This courage, which was still an option a generation ago, has lost its validity since the end of the Colonial Wars and, above all, the advent of nuclear deterrence. Today, in the event of a world conflict, we shall all die together, before going out to fight, with no more need for courage than that of a flock of sheep led to the slaughter.

We must, however, give a special place to bodily pain, which has nothing to do with physical laziness or affective fears and which—from a child's inoculation to an adult's terminal cancer—calls for courage of a particular kind.

When we are faced with the sharp pain that resists every form of chemical sedatives, there is no easy courage.

It is one of life's tragedies that we are reduced to no more than a vulnerable body. Some people learn to deal with it, others prefer to put an end to it. The sympathy of those around us is of little avail. Here we face all the mystery and violence of evil.

Each one of the kinds of courage for which we shall now envision a use has a double appellation, which recalls the ambivalence of all our life situations.

The Courage to Die (And to Believe)

As we have seen, even if death is not the most difficult thing in life, the courage to die is seminal. It is the cornerstone on which all other kinds of courage are based.

It is not even certain that the moment of my death will

demand courage. It may come in a second, amid a crash of steel plates, or during my sleep; it may even arise as a deliverance.

The appropriate courage consists of remembering that we are mortal and totally ignorant of what lies beyond, but at the same time resolving to live to the fullest. We must look death in the face and bear with our anxiety.

And how are we to do it? There is nothing new about it; when we are up against such an absolute, only another absolute can be our reply. And an absolute has no exceptions; it cannot be called into question. Man's only response to his own death must be an act of unlimited faith (for anxiety filters in through the slightest crevice).

Faith in what? It is a strictly personal affair whether you choose immortality, reincarnation, nothingness, or a return to the Infinite. The important thing is to make a choice and stick to it.

The barrier against anxiety is not so much the wager that we choose to make on the Beyond, but the calm and resolute belief that it is best to do so.

Not very easy, except for those who have a religious faith. But nonetheless necessary.

Hence the close relationship between the courage to die and the courage to believe, in other words, to clearheadedly face up to the absolute question.

Most of us don't bother. We go along hoping not to have to consider our mortality, giving it no more than a side glance and as infrequently as possible.

Hence we are open to anxiety, not because God is dead (those who don't believe this shouldn't suffer the same torments, but many of them do) but because of the suspicion that if God *is* dead, then life (which includes death) is not worth living.

The courage to look our death and its meaning for us in the face is the premise on which we base our peace of mind.

The Courage to Get Up In the Morning (And to Face the Commonplace)

Insofar as sleep is a replica of our dormant prenatal state, getting up in the morning involves a decision, even if unconscious, to grapple with life. Repetitive as it may be, it is nonetheless fundamental.

Not everybody finds it painful to leave his bed and dreams behind him, but when we suffer from physical or psychological fatigue this daily rupture can be a hard experience.

In its symbolic aspect (a renewal of action) and its very banality (it's the least of things) it sums up a real difficulty of living. It is not hard to understand why the survivors of concentration camps identified "getting up" as the most tragic moment of the day, the moment when they were once more seized by the horror of their fate.

The courage to get up in the morning must be drawn from everything agreeable that life in general, and this day in particular, has to offer. Its compulsory character (failing doctor's orders to stay in bed) means that the best we can do is to concentrate on the means of psychologically easing the operation.

Doctors recommend we not jump out of bed the moment

we awaken. A few minutes of thought about what will lend meaning to the day ahead is the best spur to the courage to live.

The Courage to Say "I" (And to Exist)

To be is a matter of acknowledgement; to exist contains an affirmation. In the preceding chapters we have shown that existence, vis-à-vis the Universe and the human race, cannot be taken for granted.

To say "I" is not necessarily aggressive and does not lead automatically to confrontation, although it may do so. For it is a radical affirmation, which draws a clear line between the entity that "I" am and all the rest, all the others.

The courage to say "I" means to assume the consequences, among them the impossibility of real fusion with any other group or individual.

To say "I" means to want to advance in the direction of being more and more fully myself. It is the work of a lifetime, and sometimes we may wish to take a vacation from it, and to take refuge in "we."

If we evade the challenge to exist while continuing to live, then we prefer comfort to control and passive enjoyment to responsibility. This wouldn't be so disagreeable if we didn't come to realize, sometimes too late, that the price to be paid is the loss of our life's meaning.

In principle, we all declare to be in favor of freedom and autonomy. But in practice we behave as if these were harsh benefits, clothes too big for us, and we slide into compromise, which is a bland misnomer for self-abdication.

The Courage to Say "No"
(And to Not Feel Guilty)

A "no" to the world is a "yes" to myself. In order to say "I" we must first know how to say "no." In any case, it must be quite a natural thing to do; babies learn to say "no" before "yes." But, later, education sees to it that this is forgotten. Because society and family have fewer problems when everyone says "yes."

Isn't "no" brutal, impolite, egotistical, abrupt, and generally disapproved of? However, it is also our only frail rampart against the assault of duty, responsibilities, love, friendship, loyalty, and proper manners.

If saying "no" is too much for me, I have only to consent and acquiesce and, like Poland over the centuries, to witness my partition by the amiable forces around me.

The courage to say "no" depends on my ability to bypass and reverse my guilt feelings. I must grant myself every possible chance to exist rather than give in to other people's demands. I must have a slowly developed, steadfast faith in the irreplaceable, even if fleeting, worth of my own life.

As with other forms of courage, the courage to say "no," if we practice it assiduously, turns out to be less difficult to achieve than we had imagined. Saying "no" doesn't create a social vacuum around us. Because saying "no" doesn't mean being tactless. Other people—at least those who need and/or love us truly—are quite willing to admit our right to existence.

We must take into account that "no" is more within the reach of rough, simple individuals than that of polished

ones. To have been brought up on tolerance and understanding had its disadvantages. We have to re-educate ourselves in order to renew our ties to the vital force of "no."

The Courage to Be Alone (And to Be Bored)

We are willing to admit, philosophically, our solitary state,
but on the condition of having someone else constantly
with us. Aren't we told that a man by himself is in bad
company? Don't actuarial statistics tell us that singles live
less long than couples?

Quite aside from sex there is more enjoyment, more
sharing, if we are two rather than one, more support and
security in operating as a group rather than alone. Even
Catholic priests these days are more and more intolerant of
their celibacy.

But contemporary men less and less do without the courage to be alone, for two important reasons, which we add
to those given in earlier pages. The first relates to big-city
life-styles and to growing mobility, which make, inevitably,
for greater solitude. In a metropolis like Los Angeles or
New York the majority of householders are alone. Whether
we are young, or old, or divorced, the chances are that
solitude will be our lot during one or more phases of our
life. Better, then, to explore its attractions.

Attractions there are, and that is the main and more
important reason for beefing up the courage to be alone.
The urge to fully develop ourselves, awakened by our liberation from age-old constraints, impels us to seek freedom
from the joys of "belonging." How many people do we see
around us who have amputated a part of themselves in

order to perpetuate an unhappy marriage, or who have not been able to stake out professional independence!

To insist on banishing or restricting solitude risks diminishing ourselves. Solitude holds treasures that may be among the ones we have always been looking for.

Besides, except in the caves of the Himalayas, solitude is always relative.

The Courage to Endure (And to Go On)

Because modern man is trained to solve problems and has forgotten (without regret) his ancestors' virtue of resignation, this courage may be the hardest of all.

This time it is a matter not of passing to action but of the reverse, of bearing up under the burden because we simply can't eliminate or modify it. This is the complaint of those harnessed to an uninteresting job, of unhappily married couples with small children, of prisoners. To live in low key, with the certainty that there is no end in sight, demands tremendous fortitude, or else leads to drowning or drugging one's sorrow in order to dull it.

No wonder that our picture of hell is of a place of suffering without end.

It assuredly takes more courage to dedicate one's life to a handicapped child than it does to risk it on the battlefield.

This dull, creeping, stubbornly humble courage culminates in something close to permanent physical pain; it means imprisonment in a miserable, diminished self. Long-term unhappiness is heavier to bear than tragedy, which can, at the worst, do no more than kill us.

All the more amazing is the courage to go on, to continue. For many people don't give up; they survive death camps, transcend their physical handicaps, triumph over long oppression. What they have in common is courage founded on faith in the beneficent, almost sacred, quality of their life. The same mixture of courage and belief that permits us to face the anxiety of death allows them somehow to go on living. And here cynics do not start out as winners.

The Courage to Change (And to Dance)

Perhaps it takes less courage to change than to endure. But it is necessary more often, and here is our problem. Change is the order of the day, and it leaves us dizzy. Today, far from the traditional models of a village, a spouse, a trade or profession, a home, we lead lives in which any or all of these things change, perhaps several times over. Hardly has one change come about than we feel that another is in the offing.

Yet our essential nature, marked by our beginnings in the womb, needs calm and stability. We need roots and points of reference, and the whirlwind in which we live disturbs us.

Hence the courage to change is in great demand. Perhaps, because, most often, we have no other option.

Inevitability alone does not produce courage, but we can draw from it positive motivation. Doesn't change make my life?

There is a powerful existential basis for the courage to change. Since nothing can ever replace the feeling of completeness I enjoyed before I was cast out from my mother's womb, it follows that every other source of satisfaction or answer to my needs can only be partial and transitory. The only solution is to pass from one to another in order to discover and experience the answers (none of them absolute) of which, in the end, I, myself, am the end-product.

No one else can perform this life-giving dance for me. It alone can lead me to the realization of my potentialities. Besides, afterward, the experience of change reveals benefits which we had not at first suspected. Herein is a new source of self-confidence and courage.

The Courage to Decide (And to Be Free)

A truly free individual is a living provocation. Often he is not forgiven until after his death. Because, in order to be free, it is not enough to be rid of attachments; we must make radical and permanent decisions about our life.

We know this, but at the same time we fear that it is too hard, that it is aiming too high. We embrace the principle only partially. Then we are left feeling guilty, and even resentful of our fellows who seem to be freer than ourselves.

Why is it so hard to decide? Because the real choices of my existence present risks which, somewhat childishly, I perhaps prefer not to see so clearly.

To decide clearheadedly means to take on the responsibility for my life, with constant awareness of my solitude. And so, unconsciously, we throw ourselves into life plans, whose real aim is to make certain decisions automatic or to leave them to other people. Religion, philosophy, career, fashion, conformism, drugs, marriage—under these headings fall decisions made by others—to save us from making up our own minds, by embracing a single decision which will draw all the others into its train.

This is a reasonable attitude when it comes to a host of minor choices. For decision making is a stress, which demands information, reflection, and even discussion. Everything that simplifies everyday decisions saves us worry and gives us protection. Hence the success of ready-made formulas which make homogenized decisions, or pseudo-decisions, for us: advertisements and advertised products, package tours, television programs, prearranged menus, and hit parades.

A free man may let himself be persuaded by a salesman to buy a certain make of car. But it is unwise to let too much time go by without examining our physical, mental, emotional, and spiritual life in order to find out whether it is what we want it to be and consequently to make decisions.

The courage to do this is born of the guilt we feel at the possibility of our even slightly spoiling our own life. From this perspective, even if it may be hard to admit, we usually know where we stand.

The Courage to Reflect (And to Concentrate)

To make up our mind is disquieting, to reflect is tiring, especially if we're not trained for it. The body is said to be lazy, but what about the brain? How many people who are ready to jog for an hour fear the trial of sitting down quietly and concentrating for ten minutes on a problem that calls for a resolution? Few of us take the time to really reflect.

The courage to reflect is almost physical in nature, as concrete as the courage to carry a suitcase up flights of stairs when the elevator is out of order. So what are we to base it on? Perhaps on this reality: I am spending my life in an environment created by the mind, other people's minds and my own.

In our civilization physical strength is of use only for sports and emergency situations. Almost everything is of cerebral origin. It is the ability to mobilize my neutrons that determines the extent of any knowledge, my living standard, the solution of my problems, what I am able to create, and my vision of the future. It's not my whole life, but it is close to it. There is a perceptible link between the quality of my life and my ability to concentrate.

As with every exercise on arid soil, the courage to reflect depends on my motivation. If I keep in mind the rewards that reflection can give me—a first prize, the purchase of a house, the winning of a contract, the impression I make on the opposite sex—I may even come to enjoy it.

It's always easier to count on mobilizing ourself through our motivation, in this case self-satisfaction, than on the discipline required to follow up on it, in this case, concentration.

The Courage to Simplify (And to Give It Up)

As a man of today I am faced with a super-abundance of things that impose choices upon me: information, desires, tasks, appeals for my time. . . . And if a life is incarnated through action, it risks splintering into fragments of hyperactivity. The lack of time for understanding, reflecting, feeling, and enjoying is one of the sources of our infamous alienation.

When we find that we have piled up contracts that we cannot fulfill, especially those with ourselves, then the need for the courage to simplify becomes obvious.

Following the example of our predecessors and the suggestions of those around us, we thought the natural thing to do was to go after power, connections, responsibilities, diverse centers of interest, and material possessions. But just a little of each of these was enough to choke our limited capacity to handle them.

It is at this point, most often against our will, that life decisions acquire all their value and all their difficulty. If we want to make our life tolerable, we have to eliminate, and choose what to give up.

Those who went into the world in the wake of the sixties believed that "everything is possible" and "if it feels good, do it!" Sociologists say that the young of that time, now thirty to forty years old, find it hard to admit the renunciations they have had to make because of the recent economic hardships or the descending curve of their own lives. You would expect the anti-consumerism of their earlier years to propel them in the opposite direction.

Giving up is one of the not-so-happy attributes of maturity. We become more "reasonable" and prepare ourselves, unconsciously or unadmittingly, for the inevitable restrictions of the downward slope.

To start simplifying while we are still in possession of our mental and physical powers is a dynamic attitude. No connection here with the courage of disenchantment. To find out that we can get along without things that we previously thought were indispensable strengthens our self-confidence.

The Courage Not to Act (And Not Give a Damn)

To give up in advance is easier than to relinquish something that is an integral part of our life. Action is natural to us, to the point that, contrary to general opinion, inaction calls for greater effort.

To refrain from acting in order to limit the noise in my life, to feel how far I have gone and where I should go next, to restore the distant perspective from reality . . . few things in the course of a day, or even of a year, are really important.

Our itch for action fills the air and kills time.

By failing to act, by refusing to concern myself with the majority of the messages that bombard me, by eschewing useless words and fleeing from triviality, I return to myself. But for some of us, this encounter is disquieting; we are afraid of being bored and redouble our activity. This craving clogs the affect just as greediness clogs and fattens the body. Too bad that the excess fat of the soul can't be seen in the mirror!

The Courage to Face Complexity (And to Ignore It)

The courage to face complexity is not contradictory to the courage to simplify. The latter aims to lighten our life, but it does not alter the fact that complexity is a characteristic of reality and of ourselves.

We all know too well that complexity is frightening and that is why we try to simplify and even to schematize things before we dare to act upon them. Afterward, action, in choosing one path for us among the innumerable possibilities, contributes to weeding out reality.

But to outwit complexity changes nothing. To forget its existence is to reduce the world to those mere outlines that make it more manageable. Here is another example of taking the map for the city.

This difficulty constantly plays tricks on us. We can't act without simplifying, but we can't simplify without abstracting and reducing. The latter procedure has lamentable effects. First, some people do not lend themselves to being pigeonholed so easily; second, some ideas are doomed to failure to the extent that we have not taken into account complexities and ramifications.

The most extreme denial of complexity is that of the totalitarians, which leads to tyranny and ends in bloodshed. Hitler, Stalin, and Pol Pot had too simple an idea of reality and human nature. The results were tragic because these leaders seized the means of putting their ideas into effect. Complexity defied them, and they set about, in their fashion, to reduce it.

The courage to accept complexity is based on the courage to recognize our fundamental ignorance without being paralyzed by it.

I am not speaking of our inadequate culture, our abysmal lack of knowledge. Obviously, we would be better off to admit that we know nothing and, before we act, to try to get a little information.

The more fundamental kinds of ignorance, however, are existential, inherent in human life, and therefore information is no cure for them. Even if we make some rough guesses, for practical purposes we shall never really know about:

· Our impact on reality
· What other people are thinking
· The causal link between one event and another
· The relative importance of problems
· The way we function inside
· What we are doing in the Universe
· What the future holds in store
· When we shall die

Let alone the great questions about the nature of the Universe and what happens to us after death.

If we admit that we are essentially and functionally ignorant, we can tackle complexity from a healthier basis. We know practically nothing, and it's perfectly normal; everybody's in the same boat. Keeping this in mind makes us, at the minimum, realistic.

The Courage to Make Mistakes (And to Hurt Others)

It is clear from what we have said that doubt perennially assaults us. When we are impelled to act we must make decisions, but because of our ignorance, these are really gambles. And yet error is disapproved of and punished, first of all by our own guilt feelings.

To face up to doubt when the stakes are high is one of the tortures we most readily inflict upon ourselves and a major cause of insomnia. What am I to do? What's going to happen next? Was I wrong? The time before, during, and after an action is often fraught with second thoughts.

Yet the courage to make mistakes is one of the noblest, combining modesty and grandeur and accepting the consequences of putting our whole worth into question.

My hardest decisions are those that affect other people. Most of us, in our capacities of parent, child, spouse, boss, customer, or simple witness, come up against them. I have to risk not only my own failure and distress but also the possibility of inflicting failure and distress on others. With the best of intentions in the world, like it or not, I can't measure the consequences of a given decision on someone else's life any more than I can on my own.

Hurting someone is not always avoidable. Our doubt, however poignant, has to be overcome. Doctors, judges, and industrialists are forced so often to hurt others that they must take recourse in one of the techniques of easy or casual courage; since they cannot lessen the impact of their decision, they must scale down the significance to them of the person affected.

The Courage to Commit Oneself (And to Love)

Freedom is like money: there is no sense having it in our possession unless we either invest it or spend it. The hero of Sartre's *The Age of Reason,* in order to preserve his freedom, refuses any relationship, affiliation, or commitment. The price he pays for his absolute freedom is total emptiness.

The theme of self-preservation, so often treated in this book, does not imply any narcissistic fixation. If we have spoken of liberation, it is because many of our habits and commitments do not give us any real satisfaction. Nevertheless, it is by virtue of the contracts we make (love and work, for instance) and our projects that our freedom can be used to produce life, aliveness.

The fact that, in our generation, both love and jobs are much more transient than before deprives us of some of the satisfaction which we still expect from them.

If love can't last, then I take care not to get too involved, in order to protect myself in case of breakups. But, in holding back my love, I make a breakup all the more likely. The courage to love is based on the courage to risk suffering in case of failure.

Likewise, to shirk living up to my professional or creative possibilities for fear of tedious obligations (business trips, going back to school, a more circumscribed private life) will set the stage for future regret.

There is a burning guilt in the feeling that, out of cowardice, I did not play all the cards that life put into my hand. A guaranteed recipe for an embittered old age.

The Courage to Grow Old (And to Stay Young)

In our day we live to be older and we age less happily. Since the dominant culture is that of youth (extended as far as age forty), growing old makes us feel more and more out of place.

The breakup of the ancestral family, in which several generations used to live under the same roof, and the attempt to ignore death make old people into nuisances and old age something to be feared. Since we do not yet have any good physical and psychological models for growing old, we see two mistaken approaches take hold; the first a pathetic attempt to ape the young, the second a tendency to let go and give up.

Since old age is becoming longer and longer, we must cultivate it like a garden, accept it without passive resignation, and keep up without hanging on.

Here we have a double courage. First we must take into account the diminution of our physical and mental powers without falling into depression. A sad old man is more often than not the author of his own isolation. He thinks it's because he's old, but actually it's because he's downcast. A smiling and affable old man actually attracts young people.

We must have, also, the courage to work and to stay alert. To eat less, while continuing to stretch the mind and body. There is no need for retirement from good looks. To remain attractive is a simple matter of courtesy in a world where good grooming is a universal possibility, available to all. Here is the courage to die young . . . as late as possible.

The Courage to Grandeur (And of Laughter)

Even if the Universe were to crush him, said Pascal, Man is nobler than the Universe because he *knows* that he is dying. And, in a more familiar vein, from Colette, "I've had a wonderful life. My only regret is not having realized it earlier."

Everything is played out, for all of us, at the level of awareness.

My dog is at my feet. Like me and probably before me, he will die. But we can't say that his is a tragic fate.

If there is a tragic element in my life it is in the measure in which, alive, I know that I must die and, dying, I know that I could have lived longer.

This awareness of my fate, whether I want it or not, endows my life with grandeur. I may as well want it.

This type of courage does not relate to the search for grandeur—which is ours from birth. But we mustn't lose it by lowering ourselves. If the will to exist turns into egoism, if our daily routine becomes trivial, we are impoverishing ourselves.

Since we are thrown, without our asking, into the adventure of life and know that it is going to end, what have we to lose by playing it out fully and generously? And if, from time to time, the heart staggers, the quickest way to bolster it is in the insolent laughter of the feeble creature face to face with the Infinite.

14. *The Return*

A ND SO, VERY DISCREETLY, even if everyone
doesn't know it, courage has come back to us. Apparently, modern society still suffers from uncertain, often
disquieting, morals. But the dust raised by the great col-
lapses, the great battles, the great disappointments, has
begun to settle.

We begin to see unmistakable signs among certain intellectuals; a new interest in individualism, which for so long
was described at least in Europe as the antisocial attitude
par excellence.

Among politicians of every stripe catchy hymns are sung
to individual freedom, the market economy, the irreplace-
ability of private initiative.

Deeper down, among a growing number of ordinary
people, we see a multiplication of enterprises and creations,
a willingness to take risks and to attack problems. Never

have there been so many declared intentions of striking out on one's own.

The fuel of these dynamic attitudes is courage.

Our book has tried to sketch its new face, so that we can all make daily use of it, that we may recognize it when we see it, and that it may become familiar to us.

The essence of what our journey has enabled us to recognize can be summed up in four questions: Where is courage? Of what use is it? Why has it come back? How can we best have access to it?

Where is courage?

In the passage to action, in the irreplaceable moment when we leave the inner world of imagination and potentiality and enter reality.

This is why courage plays a part in every action, without being necessarily difficult or painful. Its existence is almost automatic, since no action takes place without an entering into reality, and courage is the door.

But in order to set anything into motion we first have to overcome inertia. Courage, in small measure or large, allows us to overcome the reluctance of body or mind when, as is sometimes the case, reality is not so attractive that we wish to frequent it. Courage is the energy which permits us to act *in spite of* physical laziness or psychological fears.

Courage is the very condition of facing up directly to another person or to the world. Our intentions become decisions and our desires change into will only under the impulse of the courage which incarnates them.

What use is it?

Courage is necessary not only in exceptional circumstances, which call upon us to display heroism or to practice virtue, but also simply to exist.

Our essential solitude means that nobody else can find our niche in society for us or give our life a meaning.

The means of accomplishing these two existential tasks is the same for us all: action, which allows us to turn reality to our advantage and which, at the same time, secretes the meaning of our existence.

If action is natural to us and, indeed, indispensable, then so is the courage that makes it possible.

The *self,* deep down within us, takes shape and gains strength only by affirming its independence from the world, and also by accepting that it must remain separate from it. A procedure contradictory to the intense desire for belonging and fusion, which has been left in us since the period of union with the Universe in our mother's womb.

A contradiction, too, that can be resolved only by courage.

Why has it come back?

We thought it was lost or we didn't need it any more. In the course of the last two generations, a time of peace and growing prosperity, with the idea inherited from Freud and Marx that the individual is not responsible for his actions, we had written off will power, effort, and courage as obstacles. How much we hoped to free ourselves from them!

Meanwhile we live amid the increased solitude which the rapid, fragmented, nervous character of modern life has brought upon us. The support systems enjoyed by our ancestors have fallen apart, and it is harder and harder to enter into and remain in relationships with others.

The failure of dogmas and ideologies has left us without the moral framework which we formerly took from the world around us. And, likewise, collective solutions, at least for the time being, seem to have reached the limit of what they can give or tell us.

Finally, with economic crisis—or at least less automatic prosperity, marked by the threat of unemployment—we find it harder to find or keep pace. The individual is freer, yes, but more alone, up against a more complex and disquieting world. We feel that existence has become a matter of survival and that to this end we need courage.

How can we best find it?

There would be no problem of courage, fear, and the meaning of existence were we not dominated by our mortality, by the certainty that one day we shall die.

For this reason every kind of courage rests on the fundamental courage to face up to the idea of our death and to find our individual means of accepting it.

Beyond this, a harmonious management of affect (the domain of our emotions as distinct from our body and mind) will provide an easier access to the internal resource of courage.

Since our need for courage is permanent, we must use it at the least possible affective cost. That is, sparingly. Hence the search for a "low-voltage" courage, which facilitates our training in how to distinguish between a problem and the emotion that it rouses in us.

Of course, courage had never really disappeared. It is closely linked to the fact of our existence in the face of the world and death. But because it was less recognized, rarely cultivated, and never analyzed, every individual had to re-discover his own courage through experience and trial and error.

Today, everything goes to prove that our well-being or "better-being" is going to depend more and more on our conscious and modest search for courage.

Here we have tried to set up some preliminary bases for a search.

Postscript

THE WRITING *of this book has given me a good deal of courage, and I should like to keep it intact. I tell myself not to worry too much: if I feel that the level is sinking I can always reread my own pages.*

During the months when I was thinking out and writing this meditation on some of the great questions of life, the range of my usual preoccupations was greatly broadened. And I was helped to live through certain delicate personal decisions.

If I mention these things, a few lines before we take leave of one another, it is to confirm what you may well have already imagined: that I am at grips with the same problems as you. This last bit of testimony is not to be put under the heading of exhibitionism, but rather under that of sympathy (in Greek, "suffering with" the reader).

On the matter of death my ideas have been clarified. I came to realize that I wasn't so much afraid of death (although I don't in the least wish for it) as of not having really lived.

But the writing of these pages made me feel very much alive. Heretofore the meaning of my life had lain largely in my very small contribution to the perpetuation of the species and the transmission of a heritage of genes. Now it has been deepened by the process of personal creation. Nothing can compare to the feeling of giving birth to something that is ours and yet at the same time distinct from us.

It's not that I care about "leaving something behind me." That doesn't really matter. The meaning comes at the moment when the concentration of my feeble resources produces an idea or an object that, by definition, no one else could have conceived and carried out in exactly the same way.

The impression of having gained meaningfulness is further strengthened because through reflection on my personal experience, I have come to better understand how we function. At least slightly better.

When it comes to the Beyond, I find a thought of Tillich very enlightening. Belief in immortality, he says, is an evasion, for it delays to infinity the necessity of facing up to our finitude. Interesting that a Christian theologian, then, finds that the belief in heaven is not very courageous.

I don't see why after-death should be any worse than before-life. And I admire the courage of the Stoics, who didn't ask for sweeteners for the big sleep. However, since we must live, to believe in immortality is less toxic than to wallow in anxiety.

Of course, if we don't bet on resurrection it's harder to accept the sufferings and failures we encounter here below. But here can also be found a stimulus: since there's no second deal, let's play the best game we can.

"To lead a good life," we all want that, without defining what is *"good"* the same way. Thus, the great majority of the five billion inhabitants of our planet are still concerned with possessions. The bumper sticker that reads *"Whoever has the most toys when he dies wins"* summarizes this obsession. The human race has barely emerged from infancy.

And, besides objects, we want success. When our actions have positive results we have an authentic feeling of satisfaction. Because we are animals oriented toward action it is tempting to measure our lifetime achievement with a scorecard. But I doubt that the reading of our curriculum vitae *or resume after re-tirement will be enough to convince us that our life was worth living.*

No need to question ourselves at length to see that neither having *or* doing *can satisfy us. And what can we set above these two but* being? *A vaguer quality, which has the disadvantage of not lending itself to measurement. But it is in this direction that I pursued my search. And in the course of my writing I arrived at the simplest possible definition.*

Usually when we hear about a *"problem"* we look for a *"solution."* But there can be no solutions to the problems set by existence. The incomplete list that we drew up of our fundamental kinds of ignorance enumerated only questions without answers.

But the questions interest us nonetheless and demand *our response. Since it cannot be a solution it can only be an attitude. While growing to be more mature I have found that action made me exist more fully than did its results. Just so, when I am faced by the unknown or the incommunicable, the narrow margin of my existence consists entirely in my choice of attitude.*

The one that appeals to me most is personal dignity, being worthy.

Worthy of what? Of the beauty, abundance, and mystery of the world in which I have my place. Worthy, above all, of my awareness of the Universe, of my capacity to conceive it. As for my dignity, it is neither superior nor inferior to that of any other man. If I respect myself I place others on the same level: they are equally frail, equally noble.

No one can take away my natural human dignity except myself. I got it at birth, and I am on the brink of losing it when I fail to live up to my capacities and my ethics. There is a trap at every step, in every feeling that I choose to make my own, in every sentence that I elect to utter, in every action I consent to undertake.

It is by my attitude that I choose how to exist. And in holding fast to it, I can imagine a life worth leading. Not in terms of a final balance sheet, at the end of the road, but at every moment.

The right attitude makes the successful moment.

To preserve, damage, or lose my dignity depends on myself alone. While writing this book I better understood that my dignity's only armor is courage. Hence my conviction that courage is not a mere virtue, pulled out of the bag of commonly accepted moral values. It is indispensable as the means of preserving the dignity thanks to which I exist in the way that I have chosen.